Breathing
Underwater

Breathing Underwater

The Inner Life of T'ai Chi Ch'uan

Margaret Emerson

North Atlantic Books
Berkeley, California

Breathing Underwater: The Inner Life of T'ai Chi Ch'uan

Published by
North Atlantic Books
P.O. Box 12327
Berkeley, California 94701

Photographs by Bob Pottberg
Cover and book design by Paula Morrison
Typeset by Catherine Campaigne
Printed in the United States of America

Breathing Underwater: The Inner Life of T'ai Chi Ch'uan is sponsored by the Society for the Study of Native Arts and Sciences, a nonprofit educational corporation whose goals are to develop an educational and crosscultural perspective linking various scientific, social, and artistic fields; to nurture a holistic view of arts, sciences, humanities, and healing; and to publish and distribute literature on the relationship of mind, body, and nature.

Library of Congress Cataloging-in-Publication Data

Emerson, Margaret, 1948–
    Breathing underwater : the inner life of T'ai Chi Ch'uan /
Margaret Emerson.
        p.   cm.
    ISBN 1–55643–167–8
    1. T'ai chi ch'üan. I. Title
GV504.E44 1993   93–23809
613.7'148—dc20   CIP

2   3   4   5   6   7   8   9   /   97   96

I thank my teachers:
Kao Ching-hua and the people in my classes

Contents

Photographs

In the dream I'm swimming underwater, slipping through blue currents crisscrossed with a wavering web of sunlight. I feel so at home here that I'm tempted to try breathing— knowing that I'm not supposed to be able to breathe underwater, knowing from experience what it feels like to get water up my nose. Warily, haltingly at first, I draw a thin stream of water into my nostrils. Then reassured by the ease of it, I take long, slow, deep breaths while gliding in silence through the silken water. I feel welcome here; the water soothes me and at the same time fills me with a sense of shimmering anticipation. Eventually I break the surface and emerge, eager to tell my friends on shore that it's possible to breathe underwater.

The Dream

My recurrent dream of breathing underwater is a dream of inner harmony, an idyllic meeting of body, mind, and spirit. It's about my above-surface self coexisting peacefully with my below-surface self, about yearning to know my subconscious, become comfortable with it and meld it with my conscious being. I believe it's possible to breathe underwater—possible to live in my subconscious, to close the gap between above and below and make me all one thing.

They say the basis of Taoism, out of which T'ai Chi Ch'uan was born, is humankind's attempt to harmonize itself with nature. It seems to me the first step in this odyssey is to harmonize myself with my own nature, and the succeeding steps will follow as a natural result. If I'm no longer separated from myself then I can't be separate from anything or anyone else. What happens to part of me happens to all of me, and what happens to one of us or to any element of our world happens to all of us.

Over the last twelve years I've used T'ai Chi Ch'uan as a door to enter my subconscious. Through this door I peer downward, reach in, and draw a piece of my deeper self to the surface where I can hold it up, turn it in the morning light, examine, analyze, try to apprehend it with my mind.

This is a familiar procedure that I experience while practicing: there's a sense of sinking inward and encountering impulses, stimuli that evoke emotional responses. Sorrow, joy, pain, peace, anticipation, bewilderment—anything might float to the surface in the midst of the movement. Smiles or tears spontaneously appear on my face. It's very revealing and sometimes difficult to continue. The sequence is a barometer that tells me exactly what the current conditions are inside. I strive assiduously to acknowledge with bare honesty whatever appears. That process complete, I dive back down again to see what presents itself. At times I may seem quite empty.

This is a way of uncovering my nature. I don't permit myself to censor anything—there's enough distortion from the limitations of my intellect as it tries to describe the discoveries with words or images. Distinctions of "good" or "bad" dissolve as I become an impartial observer. I can always decide how to act on my findings but I can't decide what I'm willing to find.

This watching, listening, assimilating of myself without prejudice or preconception is the basis of the creative process as well as the creative life. As an artist I live on my dreams and my below-surface encounters. They feed my work, inform it with imagination and meaning.

This inquiry is an endless pursuit, exhilarating and often surprising. It's the process of becoming myself. I think that's what all of us who look below the surface and seek to conform the outside to the inside are engaged in: discovering who we are and becoming that person. Closer and closer every day so that there's less conflict within, more harmony, and therefore more strength. Inner battles subside and energy is no longer siphoned into them. My whole self is available to flow in one direction at one time.

As an artist I used to regard my intellectual or surface self with suspicion. It was something I had to shove aside to find real inspiration. The problem for me was that I excelled in academic subjects in school—unlike most of my fellow art students. I was organized, dependable, and not at all flighty. For a long time I harbored the underlying assumption that I couldn't be a real artist because I wasn't overtly flamboyant or diffuse. But as an adult who chose to make her living as an artist, I found out that my practicality, common sense, and self-discipline were necessary to my survival.

An analogous understanding has come to me through T'ai Chi Ch'uan. My subconscious and my conscious are the two halves of the yin-yang symbol. Together they can make a whole person, by themselves only a partial one. As I allow the content of my inner self to rise to the surface and then look at it and acknowledge it, I free myself to continually realize who I am. I believe this can't happen without the participation of the mind. The conscious observing of the subconscious has an effect on it. It's as if it is always waiting to be recognized, and without that recognition, without being released to the surface, it festers and does its damage. Even the so-called "good" emotions can be destructive if they're not allowed to circulate throughout the entire self. A continuous flow from conscious to subconscious— from mind to spirit and from spirit to mind—is imperative for maintaining good health.

This circular flow is catalyzed and enhanced by the uninterrupted sequence of T'ai Chi Ch'uan. Even the breathing, which draws air down into the center—the abdomen—and then sends it back up to the head, without ever stopping, back and forth, encourages this sort of exchange. Unobstructed movement, involving the entire self, inside and out, draws every part of me, visible and invisible, into the light.

This simple act of looking at my inner self is the impetus to integrate it with my outward life. Over time, with the constant emerging of new information, the two selves influence and imitate one another. Their embrace completes the sphere. This is what it's like to breathe underwater, and above water too.

The Mirror

This image of the mirror. It has been with me ever since a dream back in 1979. I was staying at a friend's apartment in Chicago, lying in bed and looking out a seventh-story window at one of those spectacular summer light shows put on by an overcharged midwestern sky. Ragged threads of lightning pierced silver-black clouds, illuminating first one, then another. It looked like the finale on the Fourth of July. In an instant a flash of white light burst into my dark room and hovered over the bed—a radiant impulse, oval-shaped, rocking slightly. I thought I was awake; I watched without fear, only interest. Its form and movement mimicked the antique swivel mirror on my dresser at home and it dawned: the white light is a mirror! I was shocked and thrilled by this epiphany. I barely restrained myself from waking my friend in the other room to show her my revelation.

I had been using white light in my meditation for some months—visualizing myself as the core of a large sphere made of numberless glowing filaments entering and exiting my body so that I am both source and receiver. It's an image of fundamental life energy surrounding, nourishing, and protecting. It gives me a feeling of vibrant well-being—"blissful" is an appropriate word. That August night in Chicago provided a connection—an equation—that keeps returning to me and growing in importance. It means that the destination (the white light) and the way to it (the mirror) are the same thing. The all-encompassing white light is the willingness, the ability to look at my own reflection. To look into the mirror. As a microcosm of the world, I contain the entire mystery. And I can use myself—my thoughts, feelings, behavior—as a laboratory for learning about everything else. I only have to be brave enough to look and not look away. Seeing what's there at any moment, not what I wish were there or what I'm afraid might be there.

It takes courage to pierce my own existence, to be willing to look at every aspect of myself and my world. In order to do this I have to cultivate a certain kind of detachment that ironically allows me to examine my own lack of detachment—my prejudices, fears, wishes, joys, sorrows—the whole range of my personality. From here I can work with my life the way an artist works with a medium. And knowing the medium—its attributes and limitations—is crucial to the success of the work.

Viewing my life as an organic work of art evokes the Taoist image of an elegant lotus flower growing out of the mud. It's a metaphor for my straining toward transcendence at the same time that I'm rooted in all the mess and tangle of my everyday life. Somehow, despite my flaws, my limitless imperfections, I do achieve a sort of perfection every now and then. As a matter of fact, that perfection uses my "mud" as its raw material, its source of energy and nourishment. Sometimes a bowl from my kiln, sometimes an early morning practice or a well-timed joke (and it does require a sense of humor to reconcile these paradoxes) can bear within it the breathtaking wholeness of the lotus.

In the fall of 1990 I had a dream which, as is often true for me, was more a brief vision than a dream. A voice asked me a question and I was made to understand (silently) that it was a trick question—I shouldn't answer too quickly. It was this: "Does the Zsolo love peace?" I'll forego trying to explain the origin of the new word "Zsolo" here, but I knew the words meant does a thoughtful person pursue peace before anything else—in other words, is that the ultimate goal? I also knew the easy answer was yes, of course one seeks peace before anything else. But the answer I gave in the dream was: "No, the Zsolo does not love peace. She loves truth." The intent of the dream was clear. Truth—experience—contains both peace and conflict. It's important to perceive the inevitability and even necessity of both, and not deny or ignore the presence of one out of blind personal preference for the other at any given time. The searching person is willing to look into the mirror without turning away— even when it reflects challenge, disappointment, conflict.

Life holds up all sorts of mirrors and dares me not to pretend to be something other than what I am. Being a teacher is one of the trickiest ones. The fact of my position creates an image of knowing. But students point out mistakes, inconsistencies, ask questions I can't answer, want to be shown things I haven't learned. I practice diligently, I watch, I listen, I read. Still there are big holes in my knowledge, and teaching is a constant challenge not to cover up those holes. I have to hope there's enough substance in between to make it worth their while. They make the judgment. If I try to influence that judgment with pedantry or evasiveness I've looked away from my mirror.

At least three thousand years ago the Chinese produced the *I Ching* or *Book of Change*—another tool like T'ai Chi Ch'uan that can be used to help us look into ourselves. It reflects the universal tides, the oscillating waves of change, and I can look into it not only to see my current place on the curve, but also my place before this and after this. It seems to be connected to the collective unconscious which is also my unconscious. This vast pool of wisdom is very accessible and eager to speak with me. I only have to be quiet and listen. I've noticed that more and more, when I consult the *I Ching,* it's telling me what I already know. My dreams, perceptions, instincts, and intelligence are what I use to guide my actions. As I've gotten better at looking at myself, I've discovered that my future is contained within a clear vision of my past and present.

This process of getting to know ourselves is an urgent one for all of us. How else can we design a society that reflects and enhances us instead of thwarting us? With technology in such an "advanced" state that we can destroy our environment and ourselves with it, we're in a race for the enlightenment of our spiritual side to put our world back in balance. Society's inside and outside have to mirror each other as do an individual's.

The surface of the mirror is unruffled. Its stillness allows me to see far in. T'ai Chi Ch'uan helps me to be still, even in motion. I reflect not only my own silvery portrait, but also that of everyone and everything that stands in front of me. People recognize themselves in my smooth surface. Some turn away; some persist. I stand in front of the mirror, maskless, patiently waiting until I enter the mirror and turn to see myself.

Yin and Yang

T'ai Chi Ch'uan is a dance of opposites and the ceaseless shifting between them. Weight pours out of one leg while it fills the other; an arm extends and then retracts; a delicate bird is held between the palms and another soars solo against a white mountain. The sequence is a collage of contrasts on every level—physical and mental, visible and invisible. It's a repetitive pattern of circling change that in the minutes it takes to complete provides me with a private screening of the forces that give rise to the universe—T'ai Chi—complementary opposites coming together to form the whole.

What we Americans call the yin-yang symbol is at least 2,500 years old. It's known in China as the T'ai Chi symbol—a beautiful and powerfully succinct representation of the Supreme Ultimate, the Grand Terminus, the root of all existence. The circle is divided into halves. They balance each other by advancing toward and then retreating from one another. As one side, one half, one color reaches its fullest then its opposite appears. It's a slim beginning that progresses around into the full-blown state that gradually gives way to its complement. The two interlocking "fish"—as the Chinese see them—are named yang and yin. (On the north coast of California we're inclined to see them, one of my class members pointed out, as two mating banana slugs curled up against each other.) The small circles of contrasting color in the widest areas are reminders that the most extreme state of any condition contains the seed of its antithesis, and no condition, no matter how extreme, is ever all one thing.

This is also a picture of perpetual motion. A straight line through the middle would have indicated an inert state, but the curved line signifies that T'ai Chi is in a state of dynamic circular movement. This turning wheel throws off objects that come into contact with it. And that's why, when I practice the martial art of T'ai Chi, I'm always turning—to deflect energy along a tangent away from me. I become a "spinning sphere."

The symbol is a good diagram of weight distribution during the sequence—the gradual and continuous shifting between legs. Like pouring water from one glass into another, every increment of change, every proportion is illustrated. Balance is not a static state.

I had some problems with balance when I started learning T'ai Chi Ch'uan. In the physical realm, my left shoe always wore out before the right. I could hear a difference in the way my feet hit the pavement when I ran, and when I was tired people sometimes asked why I was limping. After about two years of practice I started saving money on shoes and my footfalls sounded the same when I ran.

T'ai Chi Ch'uan has also been working on my lopsided personality. Those closest to me can affirm that I'm less impatient, less angry, and less easily flustered than I was before I began studying T'ai Chi Ch'uan. My concentration is considerably sharper and I know now the importance of paying attention to details. My anxiety over finishing tasks is counterbalanced by my desire to do a good job and the immersion in the process that arises from this. In my studio I look for a balance between the clay's qualities and my own expectations—each being of equal importance. I simultaneously "ride" both myself and my medium, asserting my will here, backing off there. I've learned to slow down and give each piece whatever time it takes to make it work. Earlier in my career I would have given up more easily or settled for mediocrity.

After twelve years I'm getting used to the endless changing and turning in this harmonic dance of yin and yang. It feels natural, easy, soothing. (I can detect the currents of the previous gesture brush against me as I reverse and advance into them.) Increasingly this pattern reverberates through all areas of my life—the inevitability, the acceptance, the exhilaration of change. I perceive it more keenly, can even anticipate it at times as I construe the future from the direction and maturity of present circumstances. The sequence discloses a primordial pattern to me that extends into my life far beyond a single hour's exercise period.

One of the interesting things about yin and yang is that even though they're opposites, sometimes it's hard to tell them apart. Before motion begins, during the "Introduction to T'ai Chi Ch'uan," I'm clearing and focusing my mind, my abdomen expands and contracts with my breath, my tongue moves forward and back along the roof of my mouth to complete the circuit of energy within my body. Simultaneously I'm dividing myself in half. From the waist down I'm heavy, solid, my roots extending deep into the ground. From the waist up I feel very light, as if suspended by a string that runs down the back of my neck and all the way to my tailbone. My upper body is poised for weightless, effortless movement.

Which part of me is yin and which is yang? Traditionally yang is defined as the active, creative, assertive, masculine side of life. Yin is the passive, receptive, preparatory, feminine side. Most people would say my lower half is yin since it is still—passive—and that my upper half is yang since it is poised for activity. But I experience my lower half as the assertive side at this point. I guess you could say that I see it as being actively passive—intently sinking my weight into the ground, spreading a maze of large and small roots far beneath me that wind themselves around rocks and clutch at heavy clumps of earth. In contrast, my upper half is passively active—it waits in a state of readiness. The reason it's so easy to argue this point is that yin

11

The Introduction to T'ai Chi Ch'uan

and yang contain one another. They are always on the verge of trading identities. And as soon as movement begins, that's what they do.

An offshoot of this pattern that I'm wrestling with now (and probably will be indefinitely) is the idea that the world—and I—

are indeed made of these two opposing but complementary forces, and that there is within my nature no defined negative or positive, no good or bad. It seems vital that I drop these judgments in order to see myself clearly and understand how I work. The mirror again.

Much of the New Age philosophy focuses on the continual experience of loving and peaceful emotions with the goal of leading a stress-free life. Feelings like anger or envy or sadness are lumped into the "bad" category while the obvious ones are labeled "good." I've been in several discussions with people who angrily told me that anger is not an acceptable emotion, that it didn't belong in the mature human psyche. Living in unremitting anger *is* destructive to the one harboring it as well as to others, but anger can provide the crucial thrust for change that desperately needs to happen.

Disavowing the so-called negative emotions when they surface is asking for trouble. It requires me to embrace and act on selected impulses while I reject and ignore others (which will eventually express themselves anyway in my body and my life). The trick is to recognize and use constructively the whole range of emotions—and then let them go. If nothing else, feelings I don't always like owning up to tell me about myself, give me material to work on—and keep me humble.

Feelings like sadness, despair, anxiety, and anger may not be good for my health, but they're appropriate responses to life in the world, as are joy, love, compassion, and humor. Besides, a long life and invariable good health are not necessarily the ultimate goals. I have friends, June and Bill Thompson, who risk their well-being every time they appear at a nuclear test site to object to the experiments. They deliberately subject themselves to physical danger, not to mention the overwhelming emotional and spiritual challenges that confront anyone who struggles with issues like nuclear war and the horrors of mass destruction. We make our choices based on what we feel compelled to do.

13

I can't divide my life into what I like and what I don't like and then pretend to live only what I like. If I'm alert, I'll see and address it all. For that matter, the whole demands to be reckoned with directly or indirectly, even (maybe especially) when I'm asleep. I have preferences and it's important for me to recognize them. But that doesn't change what's within and around me. What I want to do is hone my powers of observation so that I can glimpse the essential armature of yin and yang deep inside the complex, confusing, and belabored structure we call life. I want to understand how it works.

Change

People speak of the body-mind connection. T'ai Chi Ch'uan has shown me that these two entities are not just connected, they're the same thing—different manifestations of the same thing. What I do with my body I do with my mind, and what I do with my mind I do with my body.

One of the fascinating discoveries to come from my practice is that it's possible to perform these simple yet profound steps with my body, to slowly train my physical self to be better balanced, more centered, more flexible, more responsive, and without any conscious effort on my part all these qualities are transmitted to my personality. They're there to be tapped for everyday encounters—in conversations, in my work, and in crises. I'm more aware of what's going on within and around me, quicker to respond, more resourceful, adaptable, and effective.

Practicing the sequence conditions me to change. The foundation of the movement is a continual shifting from one leg to the other. The waist is always turning and circling. No part of the body is stationary, no muscle unmoving. T'ai Chi Ch'uan leads me from one opposite to another—from advance to retreat, from lead to follow, from fierce to gentle—and shows me how to make graceful transitions between them. It also trains me to be alert to the different characters of these experiences and to the varied attitudes and inner responses they trigger. This sensitivity and openness toward change have slowly penetrated my whole life. The "flexibility training" that I get through my practice breaks down the rigidity that seems to build with age, as well as the fear of change that accompanies it.

Ironically, flexibility is the quality I cultivate in myself so that I can be rigid about certain things. There are ideals and dreams I won't back away from, and finding ways to realize these things in my life is the mother of invention. Imagination, adaptability, and resourceful persistence are required to be true to any internal commitment.

Since my inner self is constantly changing, and my outer physical self as well as my personality are reflections of this core, they have to be in a continual state of transformation, too. In a sense the way of T'ai Chi Ch'uan is the easy way—it's finding and following the path of least resistance within myself and molding my outer self to it. But the "easy way" requires courage. As often as not my evolution takes me away from conformity. The study of T'ai Chi Ch'uan is not for the timid. I have to be willing to follow myself, adhere to myself.

I've decided the mid-life crisis phenomenon is the result of people taking a wrong turn away from themselves in their late teens or early twenties, or sticking with what used to be a right path much too long. These life decisions are dictated by people's outside selves (or worse yet, someone else altogether) without consulting the person within. Then, around forty, they run out of steam because their way of life has drawn more from them than it has returned. Also this seems to be a time when a person's true self breaks the surface and asserts itself if it hasn't already. The result is sudden and massive change—often very destructive—because smaller adjustments along the way were put off.

It's tempting to try to keep things the same. But I can't hold onto exterior structures after they cease to echo my interior self. People around me almost always prefer that I go on doing what I'm doing, being what I am, since they may be using me to provide what they think is a necessary ingredient in their own lives. And they're also trying to keep themselves the same. I do my best to follow through on responsibilities to other people, and this can call for some dynamic balancing between the inevitable change within and the need I and other people have for sameness. Always my life is being destroyed and rebuilt. This is exciting and challenging and, in its way, an effortless manner of living. In the end I want to be true to myself and juggle this with a life in connection with other people.

The Image

Many of T'ai Chi Ch'uan's movements have poetic or graphic names like "Dashing Wild Horse Blowing the Mane" or "Swift Blow into Both Ears" that carry with them an image complementary to the gesture. Each one elicits an inner experience with its own distinct character. A gentle movement is placed next to a fierce one, a movement of advancing next to one of withdrawing. At the same time that my weight is transferring from left to right, my imagination is traveling from one impression to another—inside and outside in harmony, reinforcing each other. My teacher told me to pretend there were yards of vivid, featherlight silk attached to my arms, billowing and fluttering in the currents I created. It's a compelling vision whose gracefulness is irresistible—it inspires me to feel and be graceful.

T'ai Chi Ch'uan is an exercise in visualization. It gives me daily practice in imagining and strengthens that skill the same as wedging clay builds muscles in my arms. During the "Introduction" I stand unmoving, using these moments to clear my mind and prepare to turn it over to the cascading images evoked by the movements. The other twenty-three hours of the day can be devoted to wrestling with problems such as how to modify a glaze formula, an upcoming insurance bill, or an argument with a friend. For this time I will be with the sequence. And I know from experience that this time apart, this brief period of releasing my grip, will somehow smooth the tangles and open up creative possibilities when I do grab hold again.

Embracing the Tail of the Jumping Sparrow

Early in the series "Embracing the Tail of the Jumping Sparrow" suggests the holding of a small bird within my hands. I have to be careful not to grasp it too tightly for fear of injuring it, yet I don't want it to escape. It's a caring and careful feeling. This contrasts with "Stretch the Wings of the White Mountain

Stretching the Wings of the White Mountain Bird

Bird" which appears a little later in the sequence. A more ven-
turesome creature, this one soars as high as the mountains, and
the arm movements are at eye level. There's a feeling of expansion
and boldness as I unfold my wings. Even my gaze is higher.
Outwardly the gesture is still soft and understated, as they are

throughout, but inwardly the effect is one of limitless force and potential. Each of the two birds is given equal attention. One is no more important than the other, yet my experiences are entirely different.

T'ai Chi Ch'uan's way of giving even weight to all the different emotions and intentions stimulated by the sequence is one of its means of contributing to balance on all levels. This juxtaposition of contrasting feelings shows me that all are equally valid and necessary. Retreating is done with the same strength and clarity of purpose as advancing or striking. Each has its appropriate time.

One of the most important invisible aspects of the movement that I both imagine and experience is my own breath. It originates from and returns to my "Tan T'ien," my center located just behind and below my navel. As I inhale my abdomen expands, and as I exhale it contracts. I follow the circular path of my breath with my mind's eye from its source out to my fingertips and toes and back again. Outward, assertive movements are synchronized with outward breaths, inward-drawing movements with inward breaths. During "Leopard and Tiger Push the Mountain," when both arms are moving in concert and my palms are pushing down toward the left knee, the force of the motion is intensified by visualizing my breath, my energy coursing from my center upward to my shoulders, down through my arms, and finally into my fingertips. My hands become warm and red, fingers begin to tingle. In this way I attentively follow—and guide—my breath as it circulates within my body and without to the surrounding space.

A friend of mine who specializes in teaching visualization to cancer patients as part of their healing process told me it has been clinically proven that the body can't tell the difference between a "real" or imagined experience. Whatever we undergo mentally and emotionally is undergone by our bodies. Several years ago both of us spotted a newspaper article released by one of the wire services. It was about a little boy around nine years old who had an inoperable brain tumor. As a last resort his doctors chose to have him try imagery to combat the cancer. He was shown as precisely as possible where the tumor was and what it looked like. (This is crucial for anyone healing with visualization.) For ten minutes at a time, several times a day, the boy "saw" the growth and imagined it shrinking. This went on for only a few weeks before he informed his mother he was unable to continue because when he tried to visualize the tumor all he could see was a thin white line. His head was x-rayed and that was indeed all that remained of the mass—a scar where it once had been.

A nine-year-old has an advantage over most of us adults. We lose some of our imaginative talents as we become increasingly focused on physical reality to the exclusion of all other interconnected realities. We become artificially limited. But that ability to conjure up any reality we want is not gone, only atrophied. With practice it can regain its force and influence. T'ai Chi Ch'uan is one tool we can use to accomplish this.

Several of my students have told me they can benefit from T'ai Chi Ch'uan without actually having to do it—they only have to imagine themselves performing the sequence to restore calm and peace of mind. A woman going through a divorce was plagued by nightmares that wouldn't allow her to sleep at night. In past crises she had no control over these episodes, and of course the lack of sleep compounded her difficulties. She discovered she could lie in bed and visualize herself practicing T'ai Chi Ch'uan and this by itself was enough to comfort her and allow her to go back to sleep. A Family Nurse Practitioner uses this same technique during the day between appointments to regain his composure and clarity. Not only is the sequence an exercise in imagining but it can also serve as a form of guided meditation.

I want to make one other comment on this subject. There is something beyond the usual definition of visualization that a long-time practitioner will inevitably encounter. "Visualization" implies familiar images which can be "seen" as forms and fairly accurately described in words. What occurs during the sequence can transcend words and images to be a complete phenomenon that involves my entire being. The pictures eventually drop away and what remains are only the wordless abstract implications: increasing or decreasing, opening or closing, asserting or withdrawing. These have their effects on the wavelike action within me, and my varied inner currents join with and melt into the swells produced by wind, trees, and sky. This is why every movement can feel like a movement of the universe.

Chi

Chi is the Chinese word for the force inherent in everything visible and invisible, animate and inanimate. It stirs unceasingly within each entity and passes between entities. If chi were water it would be as if everything existed in an infinite ocean and was composed of water as well. Chi is a dynamic force; it wants to be in motion. And it carries within it the patient yet powerful drive of water.

Practicing the sequence, I notice the behavior and effect of chi in myself. It gravitates toward and gathers in my center, coming and going from there. It responds to my breath. The two seem coupled, mysteriously and intimately connected in perpetual circling motion. ("Breath" is one of the definitions of the word "chi.") Like blood, another of its connotations, this invisible life force travels to every nook and cranny of my being. It also reaches beyond the body into my mental and spiritual selves. It feeds me, sustains me, and simultaneously cleanses me on every level. Practicing T'ai Chi Ch'uan is a gradual and inexorable accumulating of chi as well as training in how to direct and use it so that I have at my disposal an inner and outer strength beyond ordinary expectations.

I believe one of the reasons T'ai Chi Ch'uan is so valuable is that it is a form of self-applied acupressure that enhances the flow of chi, even clears away obstructions to its progress. The gentle, rounded motions, the thorough breathing, the fascinating imagery, and most of all the state of loose relaxation in which only minimal effort is made, no muscle tensed, all contribute to opening the intricate pathways—the meridians—used by chi. At the close of the sequence my abdomen feels like a rubber band—swelling and constricting, pumping energy with tranquil exuberance to the outer layers of my skin and back again.

Striking slowly downward toward the ground ("planting," as it's called), chi feels like an electrical current generated from my center. It runs without effort on my part up through my torso, then from shoulder to elbow to fist and finally into the earth. Only the simple intention is required to retrieve this energy, to cause it to slide back up my arm as I turn and reel it out again toward the east.

As my hands and arms circle and circle throughout the form, the current flowing between them is palpable. There's a stretching feeling—"like pulling taffy," as a friend described it—when my palms pass close and then spread apart. By keeping my hands always in conscious correspondence and frequently facing each other, I gather and hold and move chi outside my body.

Simultaneity of movement is crucial to the building of momentum and the eliminating of "crosscurrents." The timing of my waist, arm, and leg gestures must coincide so that each element begins and ends together. Otherwise the components of my body are at odds with each other and I feel clumsy, heavy, and stiff. When everything comes to a close at the same time—upper and lower hands reach their final destination, weight is entirely shifted, waist finishes rotating, a breath arrives at its point of return— I occupy an instant of perfect, weightless balance. Poised beyond inertia, all of me rebounds without effort into the next movement. Again the feeling of elasticity.

Constant repetition of the movements over the years adds weight and power to the current of chi. Performing the sequence in its mirror image for the first time reveals how essential the training is. Strikes done with the left hand instead of the right, kicks done with the right leg instead of the left feel hollow and

Plant

weak. One of my students described this phenomenon as "no roots at all!" That's the sensation—one of disconnectedness, flimsiness. But with practice the pathways open up and fill with energy until gradually the same sort of solidity and confidence of force exist in both sides of the body.

The Wu style long form is not symmetrical and is weighted toward right-handed people—all the strikes are with the right. I seek to become as familiar with the mirror image as with the original version. I don't expect to ever become perfectly symmetrical; that may be impossible for a distinctly right-handed person who does a lot of physical work, and I'm not convinced it's even desirable. I just don't want to become progressively more and more out of kilter. And I want the benefits of chi flowing evenly throughout my body.

Every morning I experience the cleansing properties of chi. I notice it most on an emotional level. The early parts of the sequence wash to the surface whatever my dominant mood or feeling is, whether I've been aware of it or not, and even—maybe especially—if I've been trying to ignore it. This can be a painful and difficult time. But I find that as the sequence continues, this sensation dissipates. I have the impression that it simply keeps rising until it evaporates from the top of my head. It's as if a stream of chi sweeps through me and draws all the toxins and poisons—physical and metaphysical—out with it. I think this daily "bathing" is crucial to maintaining good health.

There's no quick or easy way to get rid of anger that's been festering too long. T'ai Chi Ch'uan is a slow but sure way to accomplish this. Every practice releases buried emotions, helping me to start fresh every day.

Over time I've had some fascinating encounters with the effects of chi. One occurred several years ago and makes a good case for practicing as often as possible in the same place. I was in a deserted park one morning, occupying my usual space on a basketball court. I had come to this same spot, marked by a crack in the cement, to begin the sequence morning after morning for at least three years. There's a movement I mentioned earlier called "Leopard and Tiger Push the Mountain." Both hands push downward toward the left knee in a particularly forceful gesture that draws the chi from my center and concentrates it

Leopard and Tiger Push the Mountain

finally in the tips of my fingers. The simplicity and directness of this maneuver invite my full concentration. As my arms descended that morning I was struck by an overwhelming sensation of many pairs of arms moving in just this way, cascading images, overlapping, like a cinematic special effect—successive replays of all the times I had made that gesture in that place, and of all the moving energy deposited there over the weeks and months and years. It was there for me. All I had to do was step into it and add one more.

Chi does seem to accumulate—not just within me but in the places where I and others practice. One of the reasons I value my classes is that I get to practice with a group and can take advantage of the energy generated by people who have been performing the sequence repeatedly over a period of years in the same space. Each time we're moving in harmony, creating silent, melodic currents and being nudged by them in turn so that I feel as if I'm swimming downhill. (I can experience this within myself while practicing alone. Each segment of my body is like a member of a group, and when everything moves together each part is drawn along by chi stirred by the other parts.)

The slow and outwardly soft movements of T'ai Chi Ch'uan affect all who witness them. It's as if chi forms a delicately curving breeze that caresses and soothes onlookers. A young mother in my class told me she used the sequence to calm her baby. I've noticed distinct influences on animals as well as humans. Birds forage for worms in the moist earth only feet from where I practice (as long as my cats aren't around) and deer crane their necks from the other side of the garden, watching alertly with wide brown eyes.

For a while I had neighbors with two large dogs. The female, Nancy, was young and rambunctious. The male was older and considerably calmer. His name was Cosmos. Both of them were outside most mornings while I practiced in the back yard. Nancy paid little attention to me after charging my legs a time or two and discovering that I wasn't going to play. But there were many mornings when Cosmos stood transfixed a few feet in front of me, staring as I moved in slow motion. He faced me head on and seemed to enter a trance—all four legs splayed solidly and symmetrically outward. Eyes half closed, he watched suspended until I finished. I always stood still at the end of the sequence, holding the concluding posture in order to take advantage of the inner activity and peace generated by the sequence. But the moment I stepped aside to close the practice (my movements naturally quickened, became less fluid) Cosmos snapped awake, wagged his tail, and came forward to get his pets. His response was fascinating to me and became the subject of regular "Cosmos Updates" in my classes.

I've read there's a natural evolution of the Wu style of T'ai Chi Ch'uan toward nonmovement, and my own practice over the last thirteen years bears this out. More and more the activity of the sequence becomes internal; energy travels readily through clear passages with very little coaxing from the body— it's directed by the mind and spills from an overflowing center. The movements in my solo practice—when I'm not demonstrating for students and making them deliberately distinct— are muted and muffled while my interior feels charged and full.

I should say that such experiences while practicing are my own and may or may not be shared by others. Don't look for them—I can't look for them. Often they come at me obliquely, through peripheral "vision." The only thing to do is just practice, remaining as empty as possible for as long as possible, expecting nothing.

Like everything else that occurs beneath the surface during the sequence, the working of chi happens regardless of whether I'm paying attention to it or not. My teacher, Kao Ching-hua, said I should visualize chi reaching through and around my body. Other teachers say not to focus on it at all. In any case it is there, silent and ceaseless. As long as I join the inner activity—the undisturbed mind, the image, and the breath—together with the outer, chi will take care of itself. At the highest levels the mind is naturally empty, no longer pretending to run the show. What's left is chi.

Tan T'ien

A friend of mine who is considered brilliant by her colleagues and students tells me that she can feel different areas of her brain kicking in as she thinks and reacts—one kind of impulse originating from one section and another from somewhere else. I was fascinated to hear this, partly because it reveals an extremely high level of sensitivity, but also because my responses don't seem to originate in my brain at all. Even before I started practicing T'ai Chi Ch'uan, I felt the raw material of my thoughts rising up to my head from my abdomen. The Chinese call this center of activity, this hub of the human wheel, the Tan T'ien. Specifically it's said to be located just behind and below the navel. A translation in English is "field of red" and refers to the accumulation of blood in an area that contains many crucial organs, including the digestive tract. In other words, it's my gut, and operating on "gut reactions" seems to come naturally to me.

The belly breathing of T'ai Chi Ch'uan draws my attention to this place repeatedly. The endless turning and circling of the waist and the fact that all movement starts there encourage me to "reside" there or to "come from" there throughout the sequence. During still meditation I go inside myself and sit in that silent space. Unlike the case of my friend, my brain is only the translator of the wordless messages that arise from that area. It does its best.

I believe that I've been gathering chi or life force in my Tan T'ien with my practice. Breathing with my abdomen is normal for

Raise Right Lower Limb

me now. Without thinking, I emphasize it in any challenging situation—physical or psychological—and it steadies and strengthens me. I feel better prepared and more capable.

There's a series of movements in the sequence called the "leg lifts" which are really slow-motion kicks. My balance is tested as

Raise Left Lower Limb

I stand, circle, and pivot on one leg. Some years ago I went through a period when I was particularly unstable in this section of the form. My first response was to focus more intently on my legs. This only made me more self-conscious and wobbly. Next I decided to concentrate on my arms as a distraction, hoping my legs would relax and do what they were supposed to do. This was only slightly better. Then I tried directing my attention to my center, to where I was breathing, and from where I knew I could draw some solidity. It worked. Now I regard my Tan T'ien as my "ground"—not the earth I'm standing on. This conscious awareness stabilizes me throughout the sequence at the same time that it frees me to move as I intend.

There's a Taoist practice called the "light exercise" in which I stand with back straight, knees bent, left arm extended out to the left with palm up, right arm extended to the right with fingertips and thumb together in the "lotus position" and pointed down to the earth. The object is to imagine a column of white light streaming down from above, striking the left palm, traveling through the arm into the torso, filling the entire body from head to toe and then exiting into the ground through the right arm and hand. This is intended to be a continuous flow with light filling all parts of the body at all times, but beginners almost always start at the left side, follow it through to the right, and then return back to the left palm. Consequently what's being experienced is an intermittent light existing in only one part of the person at a time. The trick to this is the same as my strategy for the leg lifts, and I've found it works with other unrelated tasks as well. I settle my focus in a glowing white Tan T'ien while I retain the intention of experiencing an uninterrupted river of light running through me. It seems an indirect route, but it works. All I have to do is know what my intention is, then look to my center.

The Light Exercise

Silence

T'ai Chi Ch'uan is a dance without music. It's practiced in silence so the inner voice can surface and be heard. The ever-present stimulants impinging from the outside—TV, radio, recorded music, printed words, films, conversation, drugs, food—keep me looking outside myself, never in. This can be particularly convenient when my inner world is uneasy, filled with threatening shadows and jagged edges. Simpler just to avoid the mirror. The sequence offers a silent, calm, transparent surface that gives me a clear (and sometimes hard) view inside, a chance to gain some useful information about myself. I've seen that it's out of this silence that my creativity and motivation spring, and even more, my peace of mind.

My practice has been steadily teaching me the necessity of silence. In my studio it has gotten so that I can only listen to music while I'm doing work that requires no decisions, problem solving, or new thinking. As soon as creative thought is called for, the music has to be turned off. It doesn't make any difference how beautiful or inspiring or calming the sounds might be. Whatever they are they can't possibly harmonize exactly with what's going on inside me at the time. Therefore they conflict and distract. The sequence has intensified my ability to concentrate and to notice those things that interfere with my concentration.

It parallels the experience with my diet. The more careful I became with what I put into my body, the more I noticed the disruptive effects of junk food, fatty meat, sugar, alcohol, and chemicals. They made me feel bad. So I ate less of them, consequently became even more sensitive, and ate even less. It's a snowballing phenomenon. Much of the outside noise I used to subject myself to was like junk food—mind pollutants. I'm becoming very picky about what I "ingest" and when I ingest it, whether it's something I watch, hear, read, eat, or do.

Silence allows me to concentrate completely. I believe one of the reasons noise is so seductive is because its opposite—silence and the keen focus that comes with it—implies a thorough commitment to succeeding. No excuses, no pretense of casualness, no flippancy. (I really care about this. I'm going to put everything I have into it. What if I fail anyway?) My increasing willingness to leap into silence and take this risk has brought big improvements in my work, along with the inevitable failures.

There's a difference between silence and daydreaming. We've all had the experience of driving on the freeway, looking into the rearview mirror, and realizing we just passed two trucks and a car but have no recollection of it. Lost in waking fantasies, elaborate and sometimes emotional scenarios, we operated the car automatically. It's also possible for me to do whole sections of the sequence without remembering—only knowing I must have, based on where I am now. It's tempting to label this lack of awareness "emptiness," but it isn't. When I'm experiencing real emptiness, my intellect stays lightly engaged—just as much as is necessary to conduct me through the movements in their proper order, without omitting any, and being alert to what I'm doing. The intellect or conscious mind has a limited role here, but it's entirely present nonetheless, like all other aspects of my being.

Once I became solid in performing the entire sequence in its mirror image, I started making mistakes in my practice. The familiar groove of the right-handed way wasn't the only groove any more. Just a few seconds of daydreaming and I could easily slip into the alternate direction. This was disconcerting to me as well as to the people behind me who were trying to follow, but it served a good purpose because it meant I had to maintain at all times my "presence of mind" since my movements would quickly belie its absence.

Thoughts will naturally wander through my head as I practice, and that's all right as long as I don't latch on to any of them and start taking them seriously. I'm always grateful for the periods of utter silence when even the stray wisps are gone. Those times are precious.

After several years of practicing T'ai Chi Ch'uan, I realized that my thinking could actually stop during the sequence. It startled me at first. I wondered, "Shouldn't I be thinking? Where am I?" Even imagery disappeared, my landmarks. I'm convinced this state—and it distinctly feels like an altered state—is the profoundest level of meditation and the door to fascinating discoveries.

Every practice session is another exercise in not thinking. I've learned that this deep silence is almost always available to me, even in the midst of chaos. I've found that I can stop thoughts in mid-sentence and not feel compelled to finish them. This has shown me the limited and merely relative importance of lines of thinking that would normally be nothing less than urgent and crucial. I enjoy this ability immensely. It gives me a sense of power, this knowledge that I control my thoughts, they don't control me. It has become a game—dismissing thoughts that normally would carry me away with them, lead me on intricate goose chases. Suddenly they look puny and ineffective—I can laugh at myself. Out of all this emerges a self apart, someone solid who is not buffeted about by every light breeze.

Within the last few years I've made what for me is a very significant discovery. When the sequence uncovers my current interior state or condition, and this state is an uncomfortable one, my mind seeks to avoid it by creating a diversion in the form of insistent mind chatter aimed at someone or something outside myself. It usually takes the shape of a current pet gripe that I've already devoted too much time to. This is a way of deflecting attention away from myself with inner noise. It used to work until I caught on to the game. Now I'm able to brush away these distracting little pests (after noting them because their forms can be instructive) and look inside again. The pointless negativity I generate in the world stems from dissatisfaction with myself. It's amusing to see myself like a little kid, pointing the finger at someone or something else instead of being willing to face my own discontent. Anything but the mirror.

This state of inner silence has grown in stature and boldness in me. I actually experience times when the silence interrupts my thoughts instead of the other way around. It vies for my attention, and seems a palpable thing that "strikes" me just as the bark of a dog or a gust of wind might. It gently tugs at my sleeve and I turn to it.

Disappearing

The next step beyond silence is disappearing. When every part of me—inner, outer, visible, invisible, conscious, subconscious—is moving in harmony, when I have no thought or purpose, only the rhythmic, tide-like movement, when there's no longer any distinction between me and the sequence or me and my surroundings, when everything inside and outside moves in synchrony, I dissolve into the universe. I forget myself. I disappear.

It's like swimming in the ocean, floating weightless and then feeling a swell overtake me. It lifts me, propels me forward, and we move together. Then I slide back into its trough until the next one. No heaviness, no gravity, no resistance. Only the wave.

A few years ago I struggled against this step. I didn't want to disappear. After all, I'd reached a degree of proficiency in my practice—why shouldn't I witness it? But this watching myself kept me on the surface and for that matter made me less proficient. It threw me off balance and stiffened my arms and legs. So if I wanted to keep making progress I had to let go of being the observer and settle into being only the participant.

This came more naturally to me in my art. I've never seen my work in "freeze-frame" like a two-dimensional photograph. I've always experienced it as an ongoing process and each piece as a point on a moving line. The preceding pieces and the future ones are contained within. Sometimes I try to look at my work as a stranger, but that never lasts long. Perceiving it in that way doesn't interest me and even seems subversive. The only way I can evolve honestly is to stay inside my work.

Several performers—actors, dancers, storytellers—have taken my class in order to lose self-consciousness on the stage. Some have a hard time forgetting their audience even when an audience is absent. I'm the same way. I apparently want to be my own audience, and I find always being on stage very tiresome. So disappearing is a welcome occurrence.

Somehow, despite all the teaching, reading, and writing I've done about T'ai Chi Ch'uan, I've managed to preserve my practice for myself. In the mornings I'm like a little kid again, playing, and no one is watching. I can make mistakes or I can navigate the sequence with perfection; I can daydream or I can be empty. I have complete, luxurious privacy and I let go.

After practicing a chant in class a woman looked over at me, smiled with relief, and said, "I forgot myself." These exercises do give us a chance to forget ourselves, to alter our state of consciousness. And we can do it without drugs. Drugs change us temporarily from the outside. Their effects are often drastic and always unsustainable. With persistence we can train ourselves to tap into deeper states at will in a gentle, natural, and enduring way.

When demonstrating the sequence to my students, I realize the best gift I can give them is to vanish into myself, cease to be Margaret Emerson and become the woman moving underwater who is not watching herself. It's the only way to show them T'ai Chi Ch'uan on all its levels. I don't get to see it, but they do—even if some of it is only absorbed subliminally. It has taken me some time and self-discipline to get to this place. I continue to wean myself of the self-consciousness, insecurity, and egotism that keep me on the surface of my practice. Each time I'm able to disappear I enter a new dimension of silence and it allows me to proceed: more adventure.

Moving Slowly

Moving slowly is the entryway to the mysteries of T'ai Chi Ch'uan. It's the cause and the effect of my inner stillness. It's important not to move at a pace too close to the rate of ordinary movement. It seems the message can't penetrate to my interior to alter my state of consciousness—no real difference is perceived and I stay on the surface. But when I move extremely slowly, every part of me takes notice and is drawn to a common point of focus.

I never wear a watch when I'm practicing, so I don't really know how slowly I'm proceeding. Fast or slow are relative terms anyway, and when I'm immersed in the sequence and everything inside and outside is moving together, there is nothing separate from me against which I can measure my speed. When I cease to exist outside myself I transcend judgment or evaluation or measurement.

It's important to stay away from clocks while practicing T'ai Chi Ch'uan. They impose a rigidly mathematical record of time which has nothing to do with the organic process of the sequence. Time becomes elastic; a half hour is like a moment. I try never to practice with a deadline. If my time is limited, I'll choose to do only a portion of the sequence at my natural pace rather than hurry through it just to be able to tell myself I've completed something. Ideally I like my time to be open-ended, allowing for the possibility of moving unusually slowly.

There was a period of two or three weeks when I found myself dancing superficially through the movements because it seemed the only thing I could do. I'd been under extraordinary stress for a long time and my concentration was shallow—it happens sometimes and I don't like to be too hard on myself. I knew that when I was ready I would settle back down into the intricacies of every gesture, and I did. I'm aware that slower is always better. Speeding up is a sure sign of loss of focus. My students can easily tell when I'm daydreaming as I lead the sequence.

Completing the sequence is not the point of T'ai Chi Ch'uan. I see it as all one piece with the beginning movement tied to the ending movement. In a sense I'm always beginning and always ending, so I can forget about those things and tend to everything in between. When I lived in Springfield, Illinois, I used to enjoy taking Amtrak to Chicago, a three- to four-hour trip. Starting the sequence reminds me of getting on that train. The tracks immediately put me in touch with my origin, my destination, and everything along the way. There's no concern for time—someone else is taking care of that. All I have to do is enjoy the trip by watching the external and internal landscapes.

There are some very interesting side effects to moving slowly. For instance, my body begins to expand. A bracelet, a ring, a headband at first become noticeable, then disturbing. They're not growing larger with the rest of me and they're constricting my being as I seem to spread out into space. This is a phenomenon I've noticed during still meditation too, and it's an indication of a deep relaxation and inner quiet. It's as if my physical and mental tension hold me in, squeezing tightly, and when the sequence releases that surface tension I escape, particle by particle, to mingle with the rest of the universe.

Paradoxically, as my body expands, my movements shrink. They become smaller and less distinct, as if the inclination is to stop or at least to move almost imperceptibly. Over the years the movement has shifted to the inside and there it has grown into a compelling ebb and flow with a force beyond anything I could express on the outside.

I know many people are contemptuous of anything slow—it suggests lack of force, lack of direction, perhaps confusion, and certainly tedium. But T'ai Chi Ch'uan is the antithesis of all these things. Why doesn't it get boring? For thirteen years I've repeated the same series of movements on a daily basis. It's infinitely fascinating because it's infinitely complex—I continue to seek out, discover, and occupy new corners and crevices. What is seen on the surface is a faint hint of what's beneath. An invisible force is being nurtured with T'ai Chi Ch'uan, one that makes itself evident in everything I do. Along with the sensation of physical expansion comes an increased capacity to notice, absorb, react, and concentrate that lingers with me throughout the day. Slowing down doesn't diminish me, it enlarges me. One of my students, Richard Kramer, put it this way: "I've reached an age when I can't go further or faster, so I've decided to go deeper."

There are some days when the movement slows so much that I wonder if it will stop altogether. This is when I become so full of some indescribable current that a feeling of suspension and, at the same time, incredible speed overtakes me. I've come up with two possible ways of putting this into words—and they seem to be exact opposites. One is that I feel as if I'm being suctioned out of my ordinary space and time and flung into something else—some existence that doesn't have place or time. Another is that some gate opens and a fantastic raw energy gushes into and overwhelms me, blotting out everything else. I momentarily vanish. This "door" may open and close repeatedly during the sequence. I feel rubbery moving in and out of it. It's an experience beyond sensation or description. The thrilling feeling comes afterward, when I return and realize I've been away. I watch for and welcome this—it always comes uninvited and unannounced. I'm curious to see more of it, to know where it might take me.

Jou Tsung Hwa is a dedicated practitioner and teacher of T'ai Chi Ch'uan. In his book, *The Tao of T'ai Chi Ch'uan*, he talks about approaching the fourth dimension through the sequence. This means entering a state of perception that adds time to our familiar space—length, width, and height. Existence on this level allows us to see the past, present, and future instead of being limited to our moment-to-moment physical plane (which Einstein referred to as "a persistent illusion"). When I read Jou's words on this subject I couldn't help but wonder if I'm getting glimpses of the fourth dimension now and then. Is it really so impossible to escape the confinement of our measly three?

About ten years ago I lay down to sleep after a phone conversation with a friend who was worried she wouldn't have time to accomplish all she wanted to in life because of the diabetes that struck her when she was a teenager. I went to bed feeling her anxiety—undoubtedly for myself as well. In a few moments my great-aunt who had died months before "appeared." She said, "Don't worry about time. We think it moves in only one direction because we're trapped inside our bodies, our bodies are aging, and we measure time by that standard. In reality time moves in all directions—forward, backward, and sideways." With that she left me. This seemed a novel way to put it—forward and backward are easy to envision, but sideways? Does this indicate alternate but simultaneous realities? Does it simply mean not moving forward or backward, perhaps standing still in time? Is it possible to reach a point when we can choose which direction we go? Can we—do we now—exist in all possibilities at once?

If matter is made, as the physicists say, of something resembling wispy filaments of light, then perhaps we *are* light and are always traveling at light's speed and thus have within us the ability to travel in time, buried with a consciousness of four dimensions which only needs to be unearthed. I remember standing still before beginning the sequence in class and seeing my white light "shadow" on the wooden floor—two legs and the start of a torso on the smooth boards and climbing the bench a few feet in front of me. Then there are the times I've observed a lingering white imprint of my finger where I pressed it to my gray plywood wall while marking the place to hang murals in my studio. How ironic that slowing down would provide the opening to see myself as light itself—the fastest moving thing we know.

Mistakes

I've thought and written and talked a lot about the importance of details—they're the substance of the sequence. It's slowing down to notice them that leads me to the rewards of T'ai Chi Ch'uan. I approach my practice with a deliberate thoroughness. Still there will always be little flaws. As an artist I'm used to this. The aberrations, the imperfections come with anything done by a human. The question is how to regard these inevitable flaws.

I watch my students forget a movement or lose their balance; I see the looks of exasperation or anger on their faces. Then the next few movements are a loss until they can regain their composure and focus. For some, the whole remainder of the sequence is affected. I see their "giving up" in the way their feet hit the floor, the petulance in their steps, or the careless flailing of their arms. Too much importance is placed on this mistake, but it's not the mistake that interrupts their practice, it's the "giving up" afterwards. They waste time with their self-contempt. They throw away a part of their practice. One small flaw is allowed to infest the following moves and destroy their integrity, too.

Mistakes will happen and it's important to acknowledge them—I don't want to repeat them. But they should just as quickly give way to what follows. I continue as if I've never made a mistake, or as if I've made so many that one more is of no consequence. Since I perceive all my practice as one big circle with no beginning and no end, I can "begin" anywhere I choose.

So I begin again immediately after a mistake. That way every practice is "perfect." I've made many mistakes and I'll make more in the future, but my practice is bigger than those mistakes.

When I was teaching ceramics, one of my students—an architect—took his work in clay very seriously. He was proficient in the use of the wheel, and his pieces had grace and beauty. But he was obsessed with any little blemish that might show up on the surface of the clay—a tiny air bubble, bump, or divot. Once he spotted this imperfection he was unable to see the rest of the pot, to see it as a whole or appreciate its good qualities. He would torture the bowl endlessly trying to expunge that one small aberration. This is fatal for a potter—especially on the wheel. Clay reflects everything that has been done to it, reveals whether the potter felt confident or tentative. And all the time it's being worked with, water is being added and the clay is becoming softer, less responsive, until it finally looks tired and overworked. I tried to get him to see the pot as a whole, accept the flaw, and stop harassing the clay before it was too late. He never listened. He preferred to see only the mistake.

When I was studying ceramics in college, I had an outstanding teacher, an older man named Paul Bogotay. He was the "grandfather" of the Ceramics Department at Ohio State University, someone who at one time had won many awards for his work in clay, although when I knew him he had recently returned from Japan and was mostly making kites. Paul emphasized to his students the importance of setting goals that were bigger than just mastering technique. He expected us to have a personal approach, some sort of philosophical motive for working in clay and for deciding to make whatever we made. Technical perfection in itself was not a sufficient goal as far as he was concerned. In the world of pottery—especially Oriental pottery—flaws and imperfections are seen as an integral part of a well-made pot. They can add interest just as variation in the color and texture of the glaze adds interest.

One of Paul's students in the masters program was noted for his competence and precision with clay. His work was admired by teachers as well as students. One day he fired an entire kiln full of his own pieces. In the cooling process after the burners had been turned off, a lower shelf inside the kiln gave way and the rest of the shelves, full of finished pottery, came crashing down on top. Not a single piece survived intact. Paul told him it was the best work he had ever seen him do.

As people, as artists, as students of T'ai Chi Ch'uan, all of us have to be willing to make mistakes in order to achieve something—in order to evolve. I encourage beginners to stay for the second hour of class when the more advanced students practice. It provides a chance to learn parts of the sequence by following and mimicking others without step-by-step instruction. It requires concentration, persistence, and a high frustration threshold. I also tell students that this gives them some good practice in looking foolish in front of a group. Obviously they won't do everything right—there will be some fumbling and stumbling while they try to arrange their limbs in the proper configurations. But I consider this to be training in shedding self-consciousness in the interest of achieving something bigger and more important than preservation of the ego.

As soon as I refuse to look foolish, to make public mistakes, I stop learning. The only way I can lead a flawless life or make flawless products is if I do—over and over again—the things I already know how to do. The only face I might be trying to save is ipso facto a false one, and not worth the effort.

Learning to Walk

T'ai Chi Ch'uan teaches me how to walk. I place my heel on the ground and then slowly, gradually, consciously allow the weight to flow all the way into my foot until it reaches my toes as they make contact with the earth. This way I pour my weight into one leg and foot as it empties out of the other limb. When the exchange is complete it begins again—back and forth, right and left. The exaggeratedly slow motion allows time for the more than one hundred bones as well as numerous muscles and tendons to adjust, to compensate, to feel my way, and to prevent me from falling over. This is the perfect illustration of what a dynamic state balance really is. If my feet and legs were stiff and wooden, walking over anything but the smoothest, most predictable surface would be courting disaster. I've learned that besides needing to be very alert, I have to be willing to move my foot in whatever way necessary to keep me on top of my feet. Wiggling, wobbling, shifting, and grabbing onto dirt with my toes are all potential means. From a distance I may appear perfectly solid, but up close an observer would see a lot of very busy foot innards working together to maintain that illusion.

When my cats were kittens they liked to walk along the edge of the tub while I was taking a bath. This was an old Victorian tub with a narrow and curved edge. I had a chance to watch these masters of balance up close when the stakes were high. I could see all the elaborate movement and minute adjustments contained in every step. The Chinese call T'ai Chi Ch'uan "walking like a cat."

Slowing down as I do in T'ai Chi Ch'uan not only gives me a chance to take advantage of all the elements in my feet available to help me stay upright, but also encourages me to notice the process and cultivate it. Early in my study my tendency was to speed up when I started teetering. It was an attempt to get past the thorny part a little sooner and to mask my ineptitude. Later I learned the more slowly I move, the more time I have to find my balance—even when my foot happens to land on the steep slope of an unexpected divot in the yard that was camouflaged by grass, or is rocking back and forth on loose cinders. It amazes me now that I can stand on one foot, pivot one hundred eighty degrees, or cover one hundred thirty-five degrees with a slow-motion kick under these circumstances. This skill stays with me when I'm walking normally or running or climbing stairs or making my way over rugged ground. I'm less likely to stumble, sprain something, or fall. The sequence offers me a way, an approach that becomes ingrained in my body and imprinted as well on the other layers of my self.

Walking is not just a matter of falling from one foot to the other. T'ai Chi Ch'uan makes that clear during the leg lifts. These slow-motion kicks require me to balance on one leg while moving. It took me at least seven years to discover the secret to these movements: never shift your weight from the full leg—the one on the ground—until the other one has touched down. If my weight moves prematurely I have no choice but to fall onto the empty leg. It sounds absurdly simple, but I wrestled with this for years before I caught on. In this way I'm using gravity to sink myself into the ground exactly where I want to be until it's time to move.

An ice skater who competed in the finals of the Olympics and fell several times during her performance said, "I just couldn't stay on top of my feet." This is indeed the issue—staying on top of one's feet. It's imperative that my torso be plumb with the ground so that gravity works for me, holding me up instead of pulling me forward or back or to one side. I need to know exactly where my weight is, and recognize the point of complete fullness that signals the readiness to lift the other foot. If I want to go somewhere, I take the center of my body there by moving my legs, bending my knees, or turning my waist. This keeps me on top of my feet.

The posture of T'ai Chi Ch'uan is an unpretentious one—straight but relaxed. The shoulders take their natural slope; absolute minimum effort is used to stand. There's a sense of "sitting" on my spine, imperturbably solid and stable. I had to learn over the years to release the tension from my neck, shoulders, back, and legs.

Posture is the first way in which we speak to each other, and I've become an unintentional observer of the way people hold themselves. It communicates—loudly—some of the basic elements of a personality. In class I can distinguish who is comfortable with themselves and who is not by the way they perform parts of the sequence. Some are hunched and bent, some are cantilevered out beyond their feet, suspended precariously outside of their own space. The latter in particular are apt to manifest their discomfort physically in the form of back pain. Generally, people with straight backs are reflecting an inner ease and confidence.

My practice of T'ai Chi Ch'uan has diminished my enthusiasm for watching ballet or modern dance. I'm acutely aware of the unnatural tension in all classical and most modern dancers' bodies. Even in the most graceful choreography I can see at its center a rigid spine and relentless strain. I feel the dancers' self-consciousness and struggle through the performance with even the most expert of them.

T'ai Chi Ch'uan shows me how to relax into myself as I stand and how to feel my way as I walk—it teaches the fundamentals of movement. I have seen in my students how a person's posture reveals his or her inner state, and I'm convinced a change in posture brings a change in personality. Someone who is expending the effort to acquire the posture of T'ai Chi Ch'uan is someone who is becoming more balanced, alert, relaxed, and graceful. These qualities are shared by both the inner and outer person. The Chinese say we should walk as if we don't know what's under our feet, and since that is often the case, it's an attribute worth cultivating.

T'ai Chi Ch'uan is Easy

This morning the air was soft—windless and filling with new sun. My arms and legs floated weightlessly, impelled by my smoothly circling waist. I completed the sequence in an instant while moving very slowly, and by the end, without trying, I had absorbed the quiet wealth of my surroundings. T'ai Chi Ch'uan is easy, and its ease is its greatest strength.

"Effortless effort." I've begun to understand what it means and what it feels like. In T'ai Chi Ch'uan it's about moving energy without exertion, as water falls downhill, unselfconsciously carrying with it tremendous force. Not only is my body relaxed and "soft" on the outside, but even internally I'm not using coercion to move chi along its pathways. I'm simply allowing it to flow, opening up the meridians and directing it with my mind and movements. It's a subtle concept. There's the suspicion that if I'm not in a state of tension I can't be accomplishing anything. I need the gritted teeth and the equivalent feeling in my center to believe that anything is happening. It's a welcome revelation that the life force is powerful in and of itself and that my puny struggle to make it so only impedes it. I just have to get out of its way.

There's a movement in the sequence called "Dashing Wild Horse Blowing the Mane." I see a muscular horse pounding across a plain and feel the overwhelming surge of the image. Yet my body remains loose and my palms skim past each other in a long, sweeping gesture powered from my shoulders and, ultimately, my waist. Nothing resists my gesture.

Dashing Wild Horse Blowing the Mane

Pierce the Bottom of the Sea

In "Pierce the Bottom of the Sea" my right palm arcs from right to left and my knees bend to sink downward with my hand.

Energy flows from my extended fingertips, instantly penetrating to the ocean's dark floor. Despite the assertiveness of the movement, I don't have to push. I simply tap the source in my center and direct the chi's path with a clear intention.

Years ago, when I first started studying T'ai Chi Ch'uan, I saw an article in the paper about an American who was the first non-Oriental to win an international Judo championship. He gave the credit to his learning T'ai Chi Ch'uan, saying that once he understood it was *supposed* to be easy, this attitude permeated his Judo practice and opened the door to a new level of skill.

There's a balancing act in my practice that consists of applying myself with sincerity and persistence without forcing myself. From day to day I invent ways to blend my current state of mind—anywhere from serene to frenzied—with my desire to learn the form and content of the sequence. I am both the leader and follower of myself. I stay alert to the different moods that influence my way of moving; I expect and allow for variation in my pace, level of concentration, and definition of gesture. But one way or another, most mornings I'm out there beside my house, warming up, looking around, making small talk with my cats, and then practicing.

There are dangers in being too rigidly disciplined. First it takes all the fun out of it, and when that happens, it's only a matter of time before I stop doing T'ai Chi Ch'uan altogether. It's important to me to practice when I'm motivated and not to make it into drudgery. I want to be eager to practice throughout my long life. The sequence is an organic thing and changes with me from day to day. I permit myself to move faster or slower depending on how I'm inclined. Sticking with a length of time as measured by a watch only interferes with the repeatedly new experience. My rate of breathing changes with my energy level each day or with the air temperature. In really cold weather I may need to breathe through my mouth temporarily if it's too painful to take the air in through my nose. Some days I decide not to do T'ai Chi Ch'uan. These are all ways of incorporating the yieldingness of Taoism with the perseverance needed to learn T'ai Chi Ch'uan. Trying to keep everything the same from day to day would put arbitrary restrictions on me that would make me uncomfortable. I know eventually I'd associate those chafing feelings with my practice. I'd stop looking forward to the sessions and—finally—I'd quit.

I can't say that I regard my life as having been easy up to now. But I do know that the results are always better if I approach tasks with the expectation of easiness—not flippancy or diffusion—but with the idea that as long as I pay attention and use what I know, a successful outcome is the natural one. This is the opposite of attacking life as an unwieldy and intimidating opponent. Fear drains energy. (I know of a volunteer firefighter who would use up all the oxygen in his tank while he was still being "suited up" for protection against the smoke and flames.) I've found it best not to presume difficulty but to anticipate ease.

Perhaps to a beginning student T'ai Chi Ch'uan seems difficult. But it doesn't take long (with practice) to learn the choreography and then incorporate some of the invisible principles so that one can begin to derive the benefits. I simply repeat and repeat, dive deeper and deeper. It looks easy. It feels easy.

Directing and following innate energy is something I've tried to do over the last twenty years with clay, so I was not a complete stranger to this notion. Still my encounters with it in my morning practices give it a new face and reinforce my desire to admit this easy, unhindered flow into every aspect of my life.

The Directions

Each morning I prepare to begin the sequence by standing motionless facing North. With the first turning of my waist and opening of my arms I look to the East. I imagine I'm holding a sphere as wide as my span and into this curved embrace I admit the rising sun. Then, turning my waist back toward the West, my right palm draws the sun with it as if to draw it all the way across the sky to the opposite horizon. The recognition of the directions has begun.

There are eight directions within the circle of T'ai Chi Ch'uan. They can be designated as North, South, East, West, Northeast, Northwest, Southeast, Southwest. Or it's possible to name them this way: front, back, left, right, left-front, right-front, left-back, right-back. Always facing one of these directions and nothing in between, knowing the other seven exist and each will be acknowledged in turn, I address this direction as if it were the only one. And the clarity of my focus informs my movement. This is a simple physical metaphor for concentration—the ability to put aside peripheral distractions when it's time to gather my attention to one task. I merge with one direction at a time.

For thousands of years powerful spiritual significance has been attached to the directions by people of America, Mesopotamia, Egypt, Greece, China, Tibet, and medieval Europe. The Native American medicine wheel is based in the four cardinal directions and each orientation has its own meaning, its own qualities and attributes. Although these vary from tribe to tribe, the essence is consistent. East is the way of enlightenment and fiery illumination. South denotes qualities of trusting innocence and openness—childlike characteristics. West is the home of introspection, going into one's own body, focusing on the subconscious. Wisdom resides in the North. The seasons also rotate with the wheel: spring in the East, summer in the South, fall in the West, and winter in the North.

The Chinese associate the color black with North, while green emerges from the East, white radiates from the West, and red occupies the South. Heaven is green and the earth is yellow. Native Americans perceive gold or bright yellow in the East; Red, brown, and green, suggesting the earth itself and the vigorous growth of young plants, originate in the South. West contains the colors blue and black and the image of water in the same sense as in my dream of breathing underwater. North's hue is white and its element is air or wind. Colors chosen by our early ancestors to wear or paint on their bodies were not just cosmetic. They evoked the cardinal directions or the primary elements (earth, air, fire, and water) and through these colors they were trying to enter into closer communion with the divine spirits of the universe. In talking with people in my class about this, I've found it isn't unusual for someone to have very definite feelings about the qualities of particular directions, especially about colors associated with them. Sometimes these perceptions coincide with one of the teachings I've mentioned and sometimes they differ. These associations should be taken note of because they teach us something about ourselves. For instance, being drawn to a particular color at some time in one's life can signify a resonance with (or perhaps a need for) the characteristics joined with it and its corresponding direction.

Native Americans believe that each one of us is born out of one direction and therefore personifies most strongly the qualities inherent in that direction. The life's work of every individual is to "visit"—to experience and explore—the other three directions, absorb their properties, and balance all four within one's personality and manifest them evenly in life. Thus one becomes complete, a "well-rounded" person. Most people stop short of penetrating all the directions. Many stay timidly within their original one, some may combine two or three and balk at the fourth.

In my own practice I've experienced a sense of connecting with each direction as I turn to face it. Although I never consciously assign characteristics to the directions, I believe that acknowledging each direction in turn opens me to absorbing the different qualities they offer. And this contributes to my wholeness, my roundedness as a person. In other words, every day as I practice I visit the eight directions repeatedly, open myself to them, and on a subliminal level take on their essence. It all distills to the pursuit of balance. The hope is that wisdom will be developed to the same degree as innocence and trust, that introspection will balance its counterpart, illumination. All four, equally weighted, keep the wheel level.

Circles

The surfaces on which I practice vary from grass to pebbles to wood or linoleum. Before I begin the sequence the blades of grass are in their usual disarray, the pebbles appear to be randomly arranged, and the wood grain or mottled linoleum have no discernible pattern. But as I sink into the revolving currents of the movements, I begin to see circular patterns in the surface of the ground. Stones and strands lose their jaggedy, jumbled look and instead flow into circles, swirls, and vortices. It's as if I'm detecting something I was unable to see before entering the tranquil state of T'ai Chi Ch'uan. The rotating of my center out to my limbs is reflected back to me in the intricately circular alignment of tiny elements.

It wasn't until I'd been practicing for six years that I began noticing this at all, and since then the patterns have evolved. First I was seeing somewhat static forms of concentric circles contiguous with one another, the outer circles no more than fifteen inches in diameter. Now the arrangements have a more dynamic look, suggesting flowing, energetic movement—currents colliding with and emerging from each other. The most recent variation on this phenomenon came when I was motionless at the conclusion. I saw large circles radiating out from me like ripples from a pebble dropped into a pond.

The circles and swirls come and go: appear, disappear, reappear somewhere else. Always on the ground—I've never seen these formations in the leaves of trees or in the clouds. And when the sequence is ended they're gone until the next time.

This used to be a rare occurrence. Now it's common. It can even happen when I'm standing still, preparing to start the movements or while doing a stationary chi kung exercise. Am I discovering something that is always there but is only visible to me when I have the characteristically sharp vision of a meditative state? Or do I project on these materials my own inner design of circles in motion? There seems to be a reciprocal effect between me and my surroundings.

One variation on this sighting is a pinwheel design—a spinning circle with evenly spaced curved lines spraying out from the center. Another way to look at this would be as a T'ai Chi symbol with multiple "s" curves. (I suppose it was inevitable.) These curves are just two semi-circles reversed and joined—they're waves.

If everything does want to be a circle, then T'ai Chi Ch'uan gives me a chance to go ahead and be just that. The Wu style is nothing but circles, semi-circles, "s" curves and spirals which are moving circles with direction and accelerating force.

Even in sitting meditation I often find my torso rotating slightly, propelled by spiraling energy. Counter-clockwise distinctly signals energy being drawn into me, clockwise movement just as clearly indicates energy is being thrown outward. As in the sequence, this impulse originates from my center.

Of course, circles are a part of my life as a potter. When I first mentioned my sightings in class, a woman suggested I may just be dizzy from watching my wheel spin all day. A thrown pot is really one continuous spiral, and in this way my practice and my work mirror and reinforce each other.

I think these physical experiences are another manifestation of harmony—my inner with my outer self, myself with my surroundings. And somehow the circularity of T'ai Chi Ch'uan helps me to tap into the unending moving circles that seem to be present in and to underlie everything.

Making the Sequence Your Own

My teacher, Kao Ching-hua, told me of a Chinese proverb about colors that says parents and teachers are blue, children or students are yellow, and the combination of the two—the achievement of the younger generation—makes green. The blend of yellow with blue is considered superior to the original blue color unless the children are bad, in which case society regresses instead of moving forward. When she and her siblings were young they teased each other about the quality of their green colors.

I see a delightful variety of greens in my students. About halfway through the first ten-week session some of the people begin to make certain movements their own. I enjoy watching the transformation as a person gets to know and becomes compatible with a part of the sequence. Gradually they create a harmonious intermingling of their own unique body and personality with each gesture. T'ai Chi Ch'uan seems to elicit the very best from us because of its innate grace and beauty. Everyone who practices assiduously will become more fluid, more balanced and stable, more focused. These qualities interact with a person's makeup so that when they coincide with strengths, those strengths are enhanced, and when they conflict with weaknesses, those weaknesses are gently alleviated. The sequence is filtered through each individual and each individual is filtered through the sequence. The two influence each other.

When I first started teaching I told people that no matter how precisely they imitated me, no one would ever look exactly the same if only because we're all built differently. Gradually I noticed more than just the physical differences. Someone's personality comes to occupy a movement, and each person's style is very revealing. Some have a cautious way, some more flamboyant, some very solid and contained, others lighter and airier. Yet from a technical standpoint there may be nothing for me to criticize in any of them.

Of course, the look of the sequence on each person changes over time as the person changes. I know my sequence differs from year to year—students have told me. Some of this comes from gaining a deeper understanding of T'ai Chi Ch'uan and just getting better at it, and some comes from my evolution as a person. Since I know my practice influences every aspect of my life, it's difficult to determine which is cause and which effect.

Every dedicated student will eventually transcend her or his teacher. The real learning of T'ai Chi Ch'uan comes through one's own practice once the basis of the sequence has been transmitted. No teacher can accompany a student on this journey. I remember practicing with an advanced class one time, facing away from everyone and being startled by an unexpected force or energy that struck me from behind. Its direction and source were clear to me—it came from Cathy Martin, someone who had been with me since I'd begun teaching. She was my first student to communicate the compelling vitality of T'ai Chi Ch'uan to me. I could feel it without seeing, and when I turned in the course of the form and watched her it was magnified. The sequence is hers. She can go where she wants with it.

Teaching

traditional method of teaching T'ai Chi Ch'uan in China is through pure demonstration. A master, practicing alone early in the morning, is mimicked by students standing behind. There's no verbal instruction and no breaking down of the sequence step by step. The student is expected to learn not only the outward physical movements but also the inward, invisible phenomena simply by observing and following. I can understand how this would work since both the inner and outer levels of the sequence are communicated to someone who is copying the movements. However, I don't think this method would go over well in this country. It's too different from what we're used to—American students expect a lot of attention from their teachers and want to have things broken down for them, explained verbally.

Two other methods, both common in this country, are different versions of the step-by-step approach. In one system teachers drill their students on an individual movement for weeks, until they're satisfied it's thoroughly understood on all levels before moving on to the next. This means that it can take years for a student to be shown the entire sequence. A disadvantage to this is that people are so mobile in this country and their time so heavily committed, the chances are good someone will not be able to stay with a teacher long enough to get the whole sequence. A woman in my class had studied with another west coast teacher before moving to northern California. She was a serious student in the other school and learned most of their sequence before discovering she would have to move to another city. She asked her teachers to show her the remainder of the movements before she left. This caused an uproar within the school. Most of the instructors felt she should not be shown the rest of the sequence unless it was taught to her in the usual slow and thorough manner. Eventually someone discreetly showed her the end of the form so she could take it with her and have the entire thing to practice wherever she went. And she does practice it faithfully.

The method by which I was taught T'ai Chi Ch'uan and that I use myself is an alternate one. Over a period of about five months someone can learn from me the basics of the entire sequence. I think of this familiarization with the choreography as being the structure or armature on which a deeper understanding will gradually be hung. Fortunately a number of people stay with the class for one or more years. As time goes on I give increasing attention to the less visible and invisible aspects. There are many layers of experience within the form and discovering them takes years of practice—it's an endless process. However, not all that practice has to be with a teacher. A teacher is needed at first in order to learn the movements and the foundation of those movements. (I don't think it's possible to learn from books or videotapes alone.) But once the outer form is known, then it begins to do the teaching itself. No one could practice seriously over a period of years by themselves without continuously learning, without the inexorable opening up of the sequence to reveal its gifts. It's natural and necessary that the student transcend the teacher.

Originally T'ai Chi Ch'uan was taught in China by three families who for a long time didn't take any students other than blood relations. It wasn't until the nineteenth century that the Yang family started accepting people from the outside and even made an effort to spread the knowledge of their art as far as possible. Now it's not only accessible to anyone in China but also to people all over the world. For a long time the "secrets" of T'ai Chi Ch'uan were guarded and doled out slowly to selected candidates at a rate determined by the patriarchs of each family. It's said a master would deliberately withhold certain key aspects of the sequence in order to retain the expertise within a very small group. This system fits well into the strictly hierarchical society of the Orient. It maintains a distance between the master and the student, and I believe is rooted in a preoccupation with saving face. An authority cannot be challenged in front of others. Any criticism or question is seen as humiliating. It's surprising that a culture can contain this sort of rigidity and also produce T'ai Chi Ch'uan—something so unpretentious and which cultivates flexibility. My own experience tells me that it's not possible to withhold any knowledge of this art once the fundamental sequence and its underlying principles are grasped. To the dedicated practitioner, time and experience bring a profound understanding. Nothing is really known until it's experienced firsthand anyway, and a teacher can't impart this kind of knowledge to anyone. The sequence teaches itself.

A refreshing difference between T'ai Chi Ch'uan and most other martial arts is that there is no required costume, no belts awarded to students as a way of recognizing levels of achievement. What shows, what is visible to the outside world, is a gradual change in the personality of the student and in the effectiveness of everything he or she does. It's an unselfconscious pursuit and there's no way for others to know at a glance that someone is practicing T'ai Chi Ch'uan or where a person is in relation to the continuum of learning. In this way the student is encouraged to be self-reliant and act as her or his own teacher. It's up to them to assess their own progress and to decide when a teacher is appropriate and when not.

There are no standard credentials for teachers, and the student has to decide whether an instructor has something to offer. I'm teaching because my teacher encouraged me to and because it seemed the natural next step. The classes are fun and even self-indulgent for me, since they provide a chance to talk about subjects that occupy my mind daily. They're an outlet, a place to share thoughts and experiences with others who are also studying the form. Much of the content of my classes is derived from my own practice in the years since I moved away from my teacher. Yet all of it is rooted in the sequence shown to me by Kao Ching-hua.

I sometimes need to remind myself of her advice: "The best teacher is a lazy teacher." This encourages me not to rush people through the sequence, to give them plenty of time to digest new information, and to approach the classes as if we all have whatever time we need to learn. I see waves of relief pass over people's faces as I tell them there's no hurry—as the Chinese say, if you don't learn in five years, take ten, and if you don't learn in ten years, take twenty. The sequence is accessible to anyone willing to persevere.

When I first started learning T'ai Chi Ch'uan I assumed there was one right way to do it, and I was learning that way. Over the years, because of my exposure to other teachers and to books and videotapes, I've discovered there is not only wide variation from one school to another and from one teacher to another with regard to the details of the art, but there is also considerable difference of opinion on the fundamentals. One style is adamant about a straight back and another allows the back to bend at times. One prescribes a particular pattern of breathing and another the opposite. One emphasizes straight wrists and in another the wrists are bent on the first move.

The late Cheng Man-ching said that three factors are necessary to learn T'ai Chi Ch'uan: talent, perseverance, and right teaching. By "right teaching" I've no doubt he meant *his* teaching, not anyone else's. The natural question that comes to mind is if respected teachers can differ so vehemently on so many precepts, is any of it valid—or is it all just arbitrary? The conclusion I've come to is that each teaching is its own path, its own form, and it's important to thoroughly learn a particular form over a period of years because it's a way into myself. The sequence is just a tool, really, that once I become proficient with helps me to explore and discover myself. The ingredient common to all the styles is the individual student and the dedication and discipline required to obtain the tool. Where we are all headed—with the diverse styles of T'ai Chi Ch'uan and with meditation and Yoga and a host of other spiritual art forms—is toward ourselves, toward the inner mirror that reflects not only us but the rest of existence as well.

Gurus

A few years ago I attended a weekend Yoga retreat. After dinner one evening I talked with two women about our experiences with sitting meditation. Both of them were devoted followers of an Indian teacher who traveled throughout the United States giving lectures and seminars. One of my companions mentioned that while in a deep state of meditation she frequently had the feeling her arms wanted to float up into the air. But she had never allowed them to do so because this was not considered correct form by her teacher. What a loss! For me this sort of thing is half the attraction of meditation. I told her I thought she was missing out on a fascinating adventure by not following her natural inclinations. Who knows what information will emerge from one's body while in a state of stillness. It's foolish to censor or inhibit it for the sake of following someone else's prescribed form. How was any form developed in the first place?

I identified with this woman's particular example because I too have had this sensation in my arms while meditating. Fortunately my training in meditation is minimal, so I have allowed them to rise and assume whatever position they chose. As I sat one morning my hands were cupped in my lap, left hand on top. The weight of my arms dropped away and they rose upward, outward, and then back toward the center of my body and down so that when they came to rest the left hand, palm down, was underneath and the right hand, also palm down, was on top. In the Chinese culture the left hand is considered to be the receiving hand, and its placement suggested to me a drawing of energy from the earth. Perhaps that's what I needed then.

On another morning my hands rose up, out, and down so that my right hand rested on my right knee and my left on my left knee. Because of the way my hands landed, the thumb and index fingers on both sides were lightly touching—the circle completed, a familiar configuration seen so often in Buddhist sculptures.

The Taoist "light exercise" I described earlier is one I use in my classes. I give specific instructions to people regarding what they should be attempting to see or imagine. The white light enters the upraised left palm, travels through the arm to fill the body, and then exits through the right arm and its downward-pointing fingers. A continuous stream. I enjoy questioning members of the class afterwards about their experiences. I know people are concentrating and succeeding at the exercise when I get reports that the light wasn't white—it was red or blue or yellow—or that it moved in the opposite direction I said it was supposed to, or someone felt compelled to turn her right palm up and her left fingers down instead of the reverse. Sometimes it works just the way the teacher says it should. But whatever happens is the result of each person's singular condition at the time. These experiences tell us about ourselves just as dreams do. The colors have meaning, the direction of flow, the sensation of warmth or cold, light or dark. To refuse these genuine occurrences, to thwart or block them for the sake of someone else's form, is a big mistake, a lost opportunity to know ourselves.

Teachers and forms can only take me so far. I use them to get a start on my own original inventions. And, of course, many of those discoveries arrived at through solitary searching are the same as those encountered by my predecessors and contemporaries—in their solitary search. The circle turns from pattern to individual components to pattern again. All forms of meditation are living, organic pursuits and should never be restrained by dogma.

An acquaintance of mine has a guru, a woman who lectures all over the country. Laura flies to various cities to hear her. During an extended seminar my friend was helping to prepare a meal in the kitchen when the guru walked in. Laura didn't know she was there and backed into her, stepping on the teacher's foot. Aghast at what she had done by trespassing on this revered person, she apologized profusely. The guru made no reply, just continued through the kitchen. This was an important incident for Laura. She gleaned all sorts of profound lessons from it. Mainly she thought the guru's lack of response was a message that these kinds of incidents were so trivial as to not even bear recognition, much less words of apology or forgiveness. My interpretation, which Laura felt didn't bear recognition, was that the woman had lived in the rarefied world of an acknowledged spiritual teacher for too long and probably had little or no experience dealing with an everyday awkward encounter like this one. I expect she didn't know how to gracefully receive Laura's apology or smooth over the jagged feelings—her own or Laura's. I'm sure it wasn't her intention, but the woman's failure to acknowledge the incident made Laura feel trivial. My friend never considered that in this instance she may have been able to teach her guru something.

There's an episode in Douglas Adams' book, *The Restaurant at the End of the Universe,* in which a space traveler finds himself stranded on a planet that is not Earth but has the same atmosphere, plant, and animal life that Earth does. He's hungry and needs to find food, so he steps out into the center of a meadow and uses a technique he learned in a class—he radiates perfect love. Soon, drawn by these alluring vibrations, a deer walks out of the forest and comes to him. The traveler snaps the animal's neck and begins to prepare his dinner. I found this shocking, hilarious, and so insightful. People can learn to come across to others in almost any way they want. The more intelligent someone is, the more effective they can be at assuming whatever shape, form, or demeanor the target audience will respond to.

I've noticed there are plenty of people who long to turn themselves over to a teacher. They want to find someone they can trust unreservedly, who will tell them how to act and what to think—someone who can remove any responsibility for decision-making on every level, from the mundane to the spiritual. This is laziness. No amount of self-denial or effort in its pursuit can make it anything else. It's also very dangerous. Someone who is regarded as a "master" and whose words sound enlightened can be very seductive. But if their enlightenment doesn't extend to their own concrete actions, then there are all sorts of possibilities for abuse of the student. Some of the more spectacular instances hit the newspapers now and then. Never should a person suspend her or his critical judgment, especially when someone asks them to by demanding complete faith and trust.

The Martial Art

Some say T'ai Chi Ch'uan can't be taught without focusing on its fighting applications. Others try to distance themselves from any connection with combat, aligning themselves more with healing and spiritual purposes. Over my years of practice, although I have never used T'ai Chi Ch'uan for sparring, I've come to the conclusion that it is—even the Wu style—definitely a martial art. For that matter, I believe life is a martial art and requires precisely the training of mind and body that I derive from my practice.

Most of us who study a martial art will never be involved in a physical fight. Even those with black belts in the hard schools will likely never use their combat skills for anything other than sparring in a dojo. But all of us need this training for coping with everyday life—for both the physical and nonphysical challenges that are inevitable and frequent. Ideally we'll use these abilities to prevent such ordinary conflicts from escalating into extraordinary ones or even into physical or psychological violence. Qualities like balance, concentration, flexibility, and fast reflexes come in handy when we're dealing with ourselves, our work, friends, family, and strangers. These are the sorts of fundamentals that are drilled into our beings on every level through the constant repetition inherent in all the martial arts. Women in particular need to internalize these skills, take them beyond the physical, in order to maximize their safety and minimize their chances of being targeted by an aggressor in the first place.

The formalized "choreography" prominent in most of these arts is a method of training the mind and body in the most effective and efficient ways of acting. In a literal, move-for-move sense, it will only benefit us if we happen to be mugged by someone who has taken the same class that we have. But the underlying skills—awareness, stability, mobility, a knowledge of how to use our resources—are what make us less vulnerable, more able to defend ourselves.

I think the most important characteristic fostered by the practice of T'ai Chi Ch'uan is alertness, awakeness, awareness—first to myself and then to the person or thing in front of me. The sequence trains me to observe carefully and not let the constant mind chatter distort what I see. This extra acuity and the ability to calmly and objectively assess is crucial in all circumstances.

I was standing on a footstool and reaching up to a high shelf for a light bulb. I lifted it out of a cardboard box with my left hand and started to lower it when it escaped my grip. I watched it fall and had already resigned myself to its loss when my right hand, which had been resting on a lower shelf, moved in what seemed like slow motion—down and then over—to catch the bulb in midair. I stood there for a moment wondering how a light bulb had managed to materialize in my hand. It seemed too easy; the usual laws of physics didn't seem to be operating. But I assume they were and that something else had changed instead. My reflexes were much faster than I thought. The most vivid impression from that incident—besides the surprise—was the perception of slowness of movement. Both the falling light bulb and my hand seemed to be moving in slow motion. I saw every detail and had plenty of time to react.

I was talking to a physical therapist in the lobby of her office building. Earlier I had placed a manila envelope and a book on the footstool beside me. During the conversation the book slid off the stool and started its descent to the ground. I barely took my eyes off her (I was very interested in the conversation) while I reached down and caught the book. It seemed natural to me and I wasn't expecting any break in our dialogue. But she stopped to say, "Nice catch!" and looked at me wonderingly. It was only her reaction that made me note how much more common it would have been for the book to hit the floor before I could get to it.

Years of practicing the sequence, moving slowly and paying attention to details, allow me to read the signs, perceive tendencies and directions, and to know the course of the falling light bulb or book. The physical conditioning of T'ai Chi Ch'uan helps my arm and hand to respond. It's as if time itself is elastic and can expand (or contract) indefinitely. Events appear to slow. I have more room in which to react thoughtfully and effectively.

At a martial arts fair a man with a black belt in Karate told me that studying T'ai Chi Ch'uan had had this same effect on his sparring. His opponents' kicks and strikes seemed to be slowed, allowing him greater opportunity to evade or block or strike. A man who studied T'ai Chi Ch'uan for two years with me went back to his Karate class after a hiatus of four years and felt he was "three times as effective" in his sparring as he had been when he left off, and he credited T'ai Chi Ch'uan with this improvement. Among other things he had acquired a more relaxed and playful approach, which meant he was more alert and effective than his overanxious competitors. Another dedicated practitioner in my class felt her experience with the slow-motion art helped her to more thoroughly understand the faster-paced Aikido movements and contributed to her earning a black belt. This increased keenness, of course, isn't limited to the physical plane. It applies to verbal, mental, emotional, and creative situations as well.

The most striking story illustrating this heightened awareness was related to me by another of my students, Tim Carter. The incident took place five years ago when he had been practicing T'ai Chi Ch'uan intensely for about two years with a different instructor. He was walking one cold winter morning with his two-year-old son perched on his shoulders. They were in the midst of a group of elementary school students, teachers, and parents who were all walking across a park in their home town. They came to a sloping asphalt ramp which is often wet from the runoff of nearby springs. On this particular morning a thin, invisible sheet of ice had formed on its surface. Tim was immersed in conversation and distracted by the general commotion around him when he felt both his feet slip out from under him and realized he was on his way to falling flat on his back. He says this is the one time he undeniably reaped the benefits of his training. First, everything slowed down—he felt he had plenty of time to execute his response. He grabbed his son's right foot with his right hand, swung him around in front of him at arm's length and brought him down on his chest just as he himself collided with the ground. He never felt the impact of the asphalt and was completely uninjured, as was his (surprised and terrified) son. It was an extremely quick-witted and intelligent reaction. What softer place to bring his son down than on top of him? And it was deftly carried out. Tim said the whole thing "felt like T'ai Chi" to him, that the movements were slow, easy, and familiar.

Every day as I sink into the sequence, my surroundings become progressively more vivid. It's as if hills and trees, fog, and even color take on a heightened three-dimensional quality. There is an intensifying of my visual reflexes. The sequence clears the way to an overall sharpening of my senses that extends beyond my morning practice and reaches into every corner of my life. It shows up in decisions I make in my studio, conversations I have with people, and in anything I do that requires me to be alert and resourceful.

T'ai Chi Ch'uan also enhances my balance. Force without balance is wasted or, at worst, destructive. Balance channels force and releases power. A strong person off balance cannot exert her strength. If I'm on balance, I'm solid both in movement and in stillness. Off balance, I falter, my gestures are weak and tenuous; I can easily be uprooted.

In my experience real strength seems to be ninety percent endurance, and endurance is also dependent on balance. Without balance I wear myself out prematurely because all lopsided movement requires greater effort. Maintaining equilibrium makes it easier for me to be resilient and persistent.

The sequence develops a loose, flexible grace and efficiency of movement so that energy is not squandered. Because the sequence constantly requires me to move my torso and limbs in harmony, it shows me how to combine several different elements artfully, with proper timing and emphasis. This is a holistic exercise that gathers in all my various components, acquaints them with each other, and weaves them together.

T'ai Chi Ch'uan builds the qualities of restraint and self-control. The juxtaposition of movements demonstrates the mutual dependency between advancing and retreating, and reveals that withdrawing can be just as definite, just as strong an action as striking. Timing determines which is appropriate. The sequence

trains me in watching, waiting, and assessing. It prevents me from habitually jumping in to manipulate people or events without paying enough attention to what action is called for —if any.

Self-confidence is also a by-product of practicing T'ai Chi

Advance (Circling Right Upper Limb) and Hesitation Step

Ch'uan. The movements emanate from my center and I'm trained to stay within my own space, to move with grace and coordination and sureness. Just learning all ninety-seven movements and being able to practice alone reflects back to me a degree of competence and self-reliance.

Practicing the sequence is a continual reminder that everything is always changing. Becoming aware of this, accustomed to it, and therefore more comfortable with it means I'm less likely to take anything for granted and more likely to watch for signs of change—to calmly scrutinize my medium, my counterpart, my opponent.

My teacher's family was glad she took up T'ai Chi Ch'uan at the age of fourteen. They noticed she was much easier to get along with, not so quickly frustrated and angered. I've had the same experience, and a grateful member of my family has commented on it. This overriding calm that the sequence imparts conserves my energy and clears my vision. An angry, flustered person is not an effective fighter.

Done with a partner, "Push Hands" is the more visibly martial side of T'ai Chi Ch'uan. As I was taught, it's used to develop sensitivity and perceptiveness rather than as a contest, although the challenge of competition is there. Two players stand facing one another. The back of one person's upraised hand lightly touches the back of his partner's. The fingertips of the remaining hands rest lightly on each other's elbows. The person designated as the leader begins to move her hands in a circular pattern, using the turning of her waist, the shifting of her weight, and the bending of her knees to widen the circle. The follower's job is to adhere to his partner—to keep his hands delicately and weightlessly in touch with her hand and elbow. This requires him to flow into the other player, to let go of his own intentions and stick to hers. The leader, on the other hand, decides the pace, the size, and the direction of the circle while deliberately trying to conceal her plans and elude her partner's touch.

Push Hands

The two people take turns at the opposing roles; a player is expected to develop equal adeptness at both. This can be a real challenge since most of us are used to operating in primarily one role and have a hard time acting out of character. Natural followers can hardly get the circle started, and born leaders keep slipping into their control mode. Push Hands has helped me to differentiate between the two roles, avoid mixing them, and perform the right one at the right time. Failing to lead when it's appropriate and beneficial for everyone, or refusing to follow when that's clearly what's called for can hinder the progress of any undertaking. And we do all have to be able to play both parts, even if our lives call for us to act predominantly in one way.

Just the fact of engaging in an activity that can be labeled a contest has a comically predictable effect on some people. The natural competitors (especially when they happen to be paired up) immediately stiffen and an unspoken "en garde!" fills the room. It's confusing to Americans who equate physical contests with brute force to be asked to take all the tension out of their arms and maintain only the gentlest contact with their adversary. As a matter of fact, only by succeeding in this can a player prevail. On the other hand, the natural cooperators can't bear to compete. Instead of trying to escape their partner's touch, they do everything but verbally inform them of any imminent change in direction.

Push Hands trains me to forget myself—to transcend my usual self—and focus only on the game. There's a time to lead and a time to follow, a time to conceal my intentions and a time to have no intentions at all—only to adhere to and anticipate the other's intentions. Instead of allowing me only to reinforce my strengths while I neglect my weaknesses, Push Hands requires me to tend to both and harmonize them with each other.

Every one of us has to be a martial artist. At times we all have to deal with people who operate with no conscience—people who will sacrifice anything and anyone to achieve their selfish goals. This person turns up within ourselves, in our families, in our workplaces. The question is what do we do about it? How do we protect ourselves, our friends, our constructive purposes? How do we neutralize her or him with out resorting to violence? There's no neat formulaic answer to this, no "chore-ography" that can be relied on to work. We have to be creative every time. And we can prepare by training in the martial art of T'ai Chi Ch'uan, by cultivating assets like alertness, fast reflexes, balance, flexibility, timing, and serenity.

T'ai Chi Ch'uan in My Life

I know of many people who took up T'ai Chi Ch'uan in order to overcome serious illnesses. My own teacher, Kao Ching-hua, recovered from a debilitating heart ailment as a young girl and was able to resume her career as an athlete. Jou Tsung Hwa, the author of several books on T'ai Chi Ch'uan, was suffering from diseases untreatable with medication—an enlarged heart and serious stomach problems. Within five years of taking up T'ai Chi Ch'uan his health and vigor returned. My initial motivation was also health-related.

When I was thirty, a PAP test came back showing abnormal cells. This is not uncommon for a woman, and a conventional method—cauterization—was used to eliminate the problem. But months later abnormal cells showed up again, at one time being interpreted as "carcinoma in situ" or cancer in place. This type of cell change is noninvasive but is suspected to be a precursor of the more dangerous version. Doctors recommended surgery but I had a very strong visceral feeling that this was not the way to go. I was amazed and infuriated at the insensitivity shown by the doctors I consulted—by their very limited, closed minded, and what seemed to me to be clumsy, invasive, and primitive approaches toward healing. (Just cut it out.) But what about the risks of the anaesthetic? What about the fact that surgery can cause cancer cells to spread or migrate? What if I decided to have a child and the surgery made it difficult or impossible for me to hold on to a fetus? And if the cause of this problem is unknown and untreated, how could I expect it not to recur? No one would take seriously any of the information I was turning up in my reading—nutritional treatments first and then a myriad of other healing techniques.

I contacted a woman in New Mexico who, according to a woman's magazine called "Hot Flashes," had led others through a healing process for this problem. I took notes each time we talked on the phone and it was through her that I learned about diet changes, herbs, supplements, visualization, colors, meditation, and numerous other techniques. At the same time I began taking classes in T'ai Chi Ch'uan, since as a physically very active person, I thought combining movement with meditation would be ideal. It was. But I also surprised myself with how readily I took to sitting meditation as well. I employed any means of healing that I could fit into my life—I used the shotgun method.

My mornings started early with running, T'ai Chi Ch'uan, meditation, and freshly juiced vegetables. I took a thermos of herb tea to my studio and ingested large doses of vitamins. My diet took a turn to vegetarian—with occasional exceptions. I was aware that this sort of approach was gentle and therefore gradual, but I also knew my body liked that a whole lot better than abrupt and violent. All I had to do was keep at it.

Over the course of three years I was rewarded with steadily improved test results until I reached a point where even the most conventional medical doctor would not have recommended surgery. I had a temporary relapse three years later after my mother died, which didn't surprise me since I grieved hard and my health was damaged in numerous other ways for as long as eighteen months following her death. My last test, in the summer of 1992, was normal.

I believe that all the changes and additions to my life combined to bring about my healing. It's only natural that they've become permanent ingredients in my daily living since a healthy entity desires to stay healthy. And none of these measures is extraordinary. They require patience and diligence, but the rewards are so obvious on so many levels that the motivation is always with me.

A seventeenth-century samurai, Miyamoto Musashi, wrote, "When you have attained the way of strategy there will not be one thing you cannot understand," and "You will see the Way in everything." Indeed, after retiring undefeated from martial contests, he became a master drawer, painter, and sculptor. T'ai Chi Ch'uan provides a way—a course or pattern—that I can use in everything I do.

My work in clay has improved immensely for many reasons. I've slowed down, become more observant and thus more critical. My concentration has intensified so that I'm more likely to "lose myself" in my work, be less self-conscious and more committed to simply making a piece succeed, whatever time or inventiveness it takes. I have a more positive attitude and more resilience— both necessities for a person working with a medium that's very breakable and subjected to an imperfectly predictable trial by fire. Often in very literal ways the graceful currents inspired within me by the ever-circling movements surface in my clay and glazes.

My first book, *A Potter's Notes on T'ai Chi Ch'uan*, came out of this inspiration as well as the thoroughness and inner calm I'd gained from six years of practice. I don't think I could have written it at any earlier time in my life, not just because the material wasn't there, but also because the inner means to write with the required clarity and accuracy wasn't there.

I owe to T'ai Chi Ch'uan the flexibility and openness that have helped me progress as a teacher—each year learning to be a better instructor in the sequence with all its far-reaching implications. Practicing reveals the relativity of everything, the importance of not taking things (myself) too seriously, and the indispensability of a sense of humor.

Where my relationships with people are concerned, I'd say the primary benefit has been to learn restraint—the value of

93

inaction when inaction is appropriate. I let people show me who they are over time. I don't try to make them into anyone other than who they are—for my own benefit or for theirs. And I'm careful to disclose information about myself or my intentions only when I judge it necessary or safe to do so. I'm more careful to assess people clearly and not rush into wishful thinking or unthinking assumptions about them. I grew up with the attitude that if I acted in a forthright and honest way toward others they would feel compelled to act in the same way toward me. It took many years and repeated disappointments to straighten me out. Honesty is still just as high a priority, but disclosure about myself I see as optional and worthy of thoughtful consideration. I try to be alert and open to people, but I do not leave myself unguarded.

In general I'm a bigger person because of T'ai Chi Ch'uan. My spirit has increased in capacity—it can hold more, experience more, and withstand more. My dreams are increasingly vivid and premonitory. I feel more acutely what others are feeling, undergoing, and even thinking. I'm more sensitive and at the same time stronger—which is a good thing because sensitivity without strength can be destructive.

From the Others

One of the things I like best about teaching T'ai Chi Ch'uan is that it attracts fascinating people—searching people—and I get to meet them. Over four hundred students have passed through my classes in the last five years, and I'm always asking for their reactions and comments. What I'm most interested in is the internal experience of practitioners and the influence of T'ai Chi Ch'uan on their everyday lives. Some tell me their stories in the few minutes before and after class, some volunteer information during the sessions, and others write their thoughts down. I've conducted private interviews with a number of individuals who indicated to me that their practice was especially influential. The written statements (often unsigned) and the confidential talks reveal more than I ever expected. I'm astonished and delighted to discover how intimately T'ai Chi Ch'uan has entered many people's lives, and how creatively they've applied the underlying principles, dovetailing with both their work and personalities. The following pages are from the members of the class.

Ritual

A thirty-year-old writes anonymously about his experiences between the ages of ten and twenty: "This will sound most likely a little bizarre, but when anxious about something, almost in a superstitious way, I would use hand and arm motions (of my own creating) to 'right the situation.' Later, when finding a particular place to sit and meditate in the woods, I would seriously go through my own 'ceremony'—otherwise the feeling of tremendous awe and my own insignificance would overwhelm. . . . T'ai Chi Ch'uan is formalizing the method I was trying to achieve and in this way is completing my circle, and this time I do not feel so out of place, bizarre, or superstitious."

Most of us lead lives that are destitute of ritual and ceremony. Little or no religious background, scattered families, and an emphasis on the material and external make it necessary for each of us as inquiring adults to discover ways and means to access the internal. Ritual escorts us into a quiet state that clears the way for our inner selves to emerge and inform us. Ritual also steadies and prepares us for challenges, harmonizes us with ourselves and our circumstances, and gives us a feeling of control over our lives. As a matter of fact we *do* have more control—gathering and focusing our attention, skills, and energy increases our chances for success in whatever we're attempting.

Sharon Greene told me she "danced T'ai Chi Ch'uan" around a beautiful old maple she wanted to paint in watercolors. She noticed details in its form and color that she had missed before, and a sentence materialized: "Dream the tree and paint the dream." Sharon's daily practice helps her to connect with nature and landscapes so she can express them better on paper. Like many in the classes, she's also drawn to the sequence because she loves to dance and the form provides an outlet for this desire. Even people who have always regarded themselves as clumsy and unable to dance get to experience rhythmic, harmonious, graceful movement—they *become* dancers. A male student says T'ai Chi Ch'uan provides him with a repertoire of movements and those movements express "incredible physical power."

In the classes and group practices the sequence is a dance we share with each other, partaking of and contributing to the combined energy. It's a known, consistent, ritualistic series of movements we can submerge ourselves in as we surrender to the peace

Some of the others

of the circular currents. This repeated ceremony gathers the common threads within each of us and weaves them together so that we can feel our connection, mysteriously, with relative strangers of divergent lifestyles.

Pattern

Olga Loya is a professional storyteller who practices T'ai Chi Ch'uan before performing to help her speak more slowly, use her body more effectively, refine her timing, and attune herself to the natural progression and flow of stories which, like the sequence, have a beginning, a middle, and an end. Her practice encourages her to explore all the rich detail that keeps her stories changing and evolving, thus maintaining her own interest over successive performances.

Another storyteller, Suzanne Connolly, uses the deep breathing practice of T'ai Chi Ch'uan to check her tendency toward quick, shallow breaths when nervous and to instill in her body "the memory of being able to move and breathe deeply at the same time."

Kit Crosby-Williams uses the warm-up exercises during her workday as a therapist to refresh and prepare herself between clients. Robin Smith, a Family Nurse Practitioner, imagines himself doing the sequence between appointments in order to restore clarity. Paulette Buckmann stands in the back of her third- and fourth-grade classroom and visualizes parts of the sequence to calm herself. Her ten-year-olds get a kick out of breaking from a demanding lesson to "rub hands together thirty-six times" and massage their faces—two traditional warm-up exercises. Paulette also uses the sequence before playing soccer. She envisions gathering strength for the competition. Even the continuous and smooth pedaling of her bike—especially on steep hills—is enhanced by the circularity of the form. Jim Nelson has used his understanding of chi to concentrate energy in his hands for loosening awkwardly located bolts that normally would require him to use a wrench. A contractor, Jim Lowry, says he pulls fewer muscles at work because the early morning practices loosen and stretch his muscles. He also feels his balance has improved— a real asset in such physical, sometimes risky work.

Maggy Herbelin is a woman of diverse interests and expertise. For the last four years she has been uncovering and using to her advantage the connections between the sequence and her various occupations. Like many of the people who take up T'ai Chi Ch'uan, she's an internally oriented person and has practiced sitting meditation for about five years.

A black belt in Aikido, she uses the extreme slowness of the sequence to help her understand how her body moves, and to watch and correct herself. (Aikido and T'ai Chi Ch'uan, its precursor, share some basic principles and gestures—turning, deflecting, blocking, and warding off.) Practicing the sequence gives her a chance to train by herself, without the pressure of competition. She's encouraged to keep her center low and be consistently conscious of it. Also she's constantly reminded that if one side of her body is in motion, the other side moves with it—one part yang and the other yin. The following side can't be left behind or forgotten.

Maggy is a dedicated gardener and sees parallels between the flow of what she calls "vital fluid" that's stimulated within her body by T'ai Chi Ch'uan and a similar process occurring within plants, soil, and trees. By understanding her own inner workings better, she sensitizes herself to the "nourishment systems," the life-sustaining processes, of other living things. Gardening requires time and patience and her practice cultivates these qualities, encouraging her not to overlook details that can make the essential difference.

She credits the overall slowing-down influence of T'ai Chi Ch'uan with opening up new areas of awareness for her. When one of her Nubian goats was lame it was necessary to spend a preliminary fifteen to twenty minutes just soothing the animal, putting her at ease, before she would allow Maggy to even lift the injured hoof to examine it. T'ai Chi Ch'uan helped instill in Maggy the tranquillity she needed to transmit to her goat.

Mike Goldsby is currently the Program Director for Family Recovery Services in a northern California hospital. Earlier in his career he dealt directly with elderly and handicapped people. Verbal assaults were common; sometimes he even had to fend off physical attacks. He feels he benefited from his Aikido background then. Now, in an administrative position, the conflicts are subtler, more complex and psychological—competition for money, political friction among colleagues, decisions of ethics. The pressure increased with his new responsibilities and he started growing an ulcer to prove it. He feels his T'ai Chi Ch'uan practice helped him get rid of the ulcer by providing an inner refuge, a source of balance, and greater spiritual strength. The sequence showed him how to break projects down into manageable segments and focus exclusively on each detail in its turn. This helped in dealing with what for many of his colleagues was an overwhelming workload. His department has undergone major and rapid evolution in the last years, and while others around him have been unable to adjust, Mike has managed to keep himself both adaptable and centered. He has at times felt the familiar movement of the sequence in the midst of a meeting or while performing simple everyday tasks. He sees T'ai Chi Ch'uan as a way of exercising and meditating simultaneously—in his words, it's "like prayer."

Lydia De Zordo, who is married to Mike, works as a therapist in an elementary school and has also studied T'ai Chi Ch'uan. She enjoyed practicing Push Hands with Mike because it informed them about their relationship—pointing out habitual ways of reacting to one another. The sequence gives her a sense of peacefulness and of moving energy. A fringe benefit they both claim is their ability to sneak out of their children's rooms at night without awakening them.

Sharon Greene also detects improvements in her parenting skills as a result of her practice. One evening after class she was practicing part of the sequence in her living room. Her two young boys began squabbling and fighting with each other nearby. Instead of yelling at them as she normally would have (and joining the fray) she persisted in her movements. Very quickly the kids' combat dissolved into laughing and playing on the floor. T'ai Chi Ch'uan had presented her with a new tack, a different way to deal with a recurring problem, and it was effective. Her boys understandably tend to frazzle her, and Sharon has discovered it's important for her to start each day off right—she relies on the warm-up exercises and the sequence.

Jim Nelson is in the hardware business and deals with the public every day. As a high-strung person with perfectionist tendencies, he finds T'ai Chi Ch'uan helps him to maintain his composure with difficult people. He feels the sequence has improved his outlook on life, adding both harmony and perspective.

Cathy Martin applies the principles of T'ai Chi Ch'uan to her work as a nurse. It helps her to slow down in tense situations, to cope with a barrage of simultaneous demands, and to pay attention to her own body—how she moves, how she lifts and turns patients, how she breathes. She's conscious even of her walking, as if it's a dance.

Cathy experiences a stabilizing effect from T'ai Chi Ch'uan that has both physical and mental implications. Her focus gravitates downward from her brain to her waist, relieving tension from her head, neck, and shoulders. With her attention residing in the center of her body she's less likely to drift off into daydreams about the past or future. She refers to this as "grounding" because it keeps her in her body and in the present.

Stress

Nearly everyone who practices T'ai Chi Ch'uan uses it at one time or another (if not primarily) to deal with psychological stress. One such person encountered the art when he was close to being paralyzed with depression following a divorce. Although instant results are not guaranteed with T'ai Chi Ch'uan and it generally works slowly and gradually, this is what he says about his initial class taught by his first instructor, Chris Johnson:

". . . I could feel benefits coming to me. I was bathed in this wonderful energy with this group of total strangers." He goes on to say, with regard to his continued study, "T'ai Chi has helped me refocus and proceed. I am transformed spiritually, physically, emotionally, and mentally by my practice and learning . . . I am more centered. I am more aware. I am less stressed, less angry, and less depressed. T'ai Chi has helped me to become more accepting of life and consequently more balanced. I am more relaxed. I am a better parent. I am a better human being. T'ai Chi is something I now give myself. It nurtures me and soothes me. T'ai Chi cannot be taken from me. I have T'ai Chi Ch'uan for life. Some of the most beautiful, most radiant human beings I've met practice T'ai Chi Ch'uan. They are inspiration." (What a testimonial!)

Lesley Meriwether, a therapist, writes, "I will do T'ai Chi for the rest of my life—somehow. It is for my mind and for my body. I often do it in my head." I think this next statement of Lesley's relates to the earlier thoughts about self-acceptance and just generally learning how to loosen one's grip and relax: "When I first started with T'ai Chi I thought I had to do it perfectly—I misunderstood—it's not about doing perfectly in the usual sense but rather in doing completely. I can accept my 'mistakes' more easily in T'ai Chi now than in any other area of my life and yet that acceptance has been extended into the rest of my life as well. This has been one of the many unexpected 'gifts' from T'ai Chi. I love the breathing, the awareness of my breath and body. I can do it without thinking about other things, just feeling it and being it. I *always* feel more energized and relaxed when I'm finished."

Rich Lewis, a forty-eight-year-old geology and biology teacher, combines T'ai Chi Ch'uan with bicycling, a vegetarian diet, and a deliberate light-hearted attitude toward work in order to maintain his health at a high level. Specifically he's seeking to control cholesterol, high blood pressure, and stress levels. Recently he was able to eliminate his blood pressure medicine with no ill effects. "Once you learn the sequence," he says, "you can internalize it, so that when something upsets you, you can go through the sequence in your mind, and it will calm you down." As a biologist Rich has had an academic understanding of the inner workings of the body, but practicing the sequence for three years has made him acutely aware of what each muscle in his own body is doing. "You need to have a lot of control, balance, and concentration." Because stress has been shown to suppress the immune system, and T'ai Chi Ch'uan can alleviate stress, he sees it as a form of mental healing. "The idea behind T'ai Chi Ch'uan," he feels, "is that you go through the movements and your mind just becomes quiet."

Other students have told me they feel the absence of the classes during breaks for holidays, in between sessions, or when they have to travel out of town. "Things don't go as well," a man told me. He also claims his practice is good for depression, that it's relaxing both physically and mentally, and it improves his digestion. A woman who suffers from allergies brought on by stress says T'ai Chi Ch'uan reduces the stress, the allergies, and even the snoring caused by the allergies. From the spiritual to the mundane, the sequence touches every level of people's lives—because all those levels are part of the same unified whole.

Physical

Julia Hesse is a good example of the many people who take up T'ai Chi Ch'uan to address physical problems. She had tendonitis in her shoulders, neck, and back and needed to find a form of exercise that wouldn't exacerbate the problem or actually injure her. I remember during her first class there were many warm-up exercises she couldn't do because she had difficulty raising her arms, and all the upper body movements were performed gingerly, in as limited a range as she could get away with. Within a couple of months her neck and shoulders were much improved

—she was doing all the warm-ups and all the sequence she had been shown. (Sharon Greene had a similar chronic problem with a shoulder and feels it responded well to T'ai Chi Ch'uan because of the enhanced circulation—she experiences a tingling sensation in the joint caused by the increased energy flow.)

Julia has studied contemporary shamanism for years, and her teachers recommended she study a martial art. For her, safe, low-impact T'ai Chi Ch'uan was the only possibility. Practicing has added mental as well as physical stability to her life. She feels more centered in stressful times and while doing spiritual work. The sequence is now a "necessary" activity in her life, "an integral part of my physical, spiritual, emotional and mental balance."

A thirty-year-old woman in my class was diagnosed at the age of twenty-eight with lupus—an autoimmune disease that affects the skin and causes the joints to deteriorate. She's highly motivated to practice because she sees T'ai Chi Ch'uan as one facet of a multifaceted, lifelong endeavor to maintain her health. She reports these results: she wears her shoes out more evenly (meaning her posture has balanced and straightened), the stress of her job as a public health nurse has diminished, and most pertinently, her joints are significantly less inflamed and more mobile.

I watched Jim Nelson's balance improve with each passing week. An ear problem that started almost ten years ago made it difficult for him to do any of the one-legged warm-ups or leg lifts in the sequence. Now he performs them easily and feels more limber as well. He also notices that his hand-eye coordination is keener. Jim used to be a serious runner until he was forced to quit after an injury. It was hard for him to give it up, but the sequence provides some of the euphoria that running produced after four or five miles.

Cynthia Ross came to class to alleviate lower back pain and what she felt was "general physical deterioration." She's also swimming, walking, and using homeopathy and acupuncture to improve her overall health. T'ai Chi Ch'uan has helped her become more aware of her body, especially of the stiffer joints that come with aging. The sequence helps keep her joints more mobile. She feels her general body strength and balance have been enhanced. Cynthia uses T'ai Chi Ch'uan exercises during her lunch break from her work as ombudsman at a Senior Resource Center to relax the tension across her shoulders, neck, and arms. And the opportunity to clear her mind allows her not only to listen more keenly while others speak, but even promotes creativity in finding solutions to problems that are appropriate to all concerned. She uses the sequence to treat colds, flu, headaches, tension, and even spasms of the throat. If she walks into class with a spasm, she walks out without one. Her practice may also be affecting her personality, encouraging her to be more positive, more open, and more flexible in times of change. T'ai Chi Ch'uan "is wherever I am and can be a tool to be used in many different ways."

I wasn't aware of it at the time, but one of my students was coming to class drunk and stoned in the first months. I knew he looked unhealthy—overly thin, sallow complexion, slumping posture. He was, however, intent on learning T'ai Chi Ch'uan— and he did. In the early stages, he told me later in an interview, the sequence seemed to release dammed-up emotions that had been held back and masked by drugs and alcohol. He cried frequently during this period without knowing why. His practice unbottled both anger and sadness, and it took self-discipline to keep coming back to it. After two months of T'ai Chi Ch'uan he had stopped drinking. The marijuana smoking had ceased even earlier, with some additional encouragement from the sight of his kids walking around the house with "Just Say No" buttons they'd been given at school.

I know T'ai Chi Ch'uan came into his life at a time when he realized he was in trouble and needed to change. He started early experimenting with drugs and had what he considered some genuinely awakening experiences, but then became "hung up" on them. When he drove off a country road into a fence post with his wife and all four children in the car, he knew he had to do something.

In addition to using T'ai Chi Ch'uan as a means to stabilize and strengthen himself physically and mentally, he also runs and practices yoga and sitting meditation. I saw his appearance transform over a period of about two years. It looked as if someone had attached a bicycle pump to him and expanded him from the inside. His face filled out, his complexion turned from gray to pink, his shoulders rose, and his spine straightened. He looks happier and more peaceful, too.

I currently have an alcoholic in the class—a new student— who is using his practice as part of a self-designed program to enhance his recovery. So far he tells me his practice is helping him to be less critical and more patient with himself, thus alleviating what he sees as a primary source of his drinking.

Cynthia Ross, mentioned earlier, has had various types of experience working with drug abusers, including two years with the Illinois Drug Abuse Program in Chicago and as a counselor in homeless shelters and in schools. She thinks T'ai Chi Ch'uan can help people rebuild their bodies—a necessary task for drug abusers—and can reduce the aches and pains of drug detoxification, which linger for many days after the drug is removed. The internal focus required by the sequence can provide a respite from their constant preoccupation with the next fix. Energies, she feels, such as "smarts," perseverance, single-mindedness, and tension—which are all used by an addict to maintain his or her habit—can be redirected by T'ai Chi Ch'uan practice to positive ends. Cynthia thinks the emphasis should not be solely on long-term benefits from the sequence. She sees immediate benefits from the first class that can be utilized by a drug abuser— increased balance and awareness, relaxation, and a new, more positive focus. She emphasizes that T'ai Chi Ch'uan is a technique centering on the individual, not a particular treatment or recovery program.

In the winter of 1992 I spoke at a conference sponsored by St. Joseph's Hospital in Eureka, California, on alternative treatments to drug abuse. The consensus among experienced professionals was that sustained practice of any of the martial arts gives people pride of accomplishment and tangible evidence that steady persistence brings rewards. The study of T'ai Chi Ch'uan asks people to apply themselves consistently over time to acquiring physical and mental skills that manifest themselves—on increasingly higher levels—with each practice. A well-trained body and mind are concrete acquisitions that cannot be taken away. Learning T'ai Chi Ch'uan demonstrates to a person that she or he can have a high degree of control over themselves and their lives.

Creativity

Michael Ferrier is an accomplished woodworker who chisels away the extraneous pieces of a chunk of wild wood to disclose the graceful, high-strung forms of native birds and animals hinted at within. Learning T'ai Chi Ch'uan caused him to rethink his approach to carving, starting at the beginning. He went back to forming simple, elegant wooden spoons—many of them, over and over—then took what he learned and applied it to the more complex creatures again. This is a sort of "learning to walk" that led him to start at the ground and reappraise his posture and stance toward his work. Then these changes, internalized, informed every step of the carving process.

Kay Schaser awoke one morning to three distinct patterns forming in her imagination, one after the other. Although she is an artist who has worked in various media, this spontaneous and unexpected appearance of unique designs was new to her. In the past developing such things has always been hard work, and she hopes that continued practice of the sequence will catalyze more such revelations. As she put it, "... it's an exciting prospect to think there might be a creative reservoir into which I could tap."

Kate Culbertson is a professional pianist who teaches students privately. She detects parallels between the flow of the sequence and the "melodic line" in music that carries motion forward. T'ai Chi Ch'uan not only gives her another way to internalize this concept but also a new tack for explaining it to students in the hopes that this might "strike a chord."

I've mentioned in earlier sections some of the others who discovered their practice stimulated creativity—Cynthia Ross' enhanced problem-solving at work, Sharon Greene's painting and parenting. Dorn Yoder, a dancer and choreographer, has distilled the essence of some of the T'ai Chi Ch'uan movements and woven their flowing energy very expressively into performance pieces. Nearly everyone who uses T'ai Chi Ch'uan in their everyday life is adding to their imaginative powers. I think this is because creativity always starts fresh and alert at the beginning, with no old assumptions or worn patterns. From there we're free to leap in any direction, according to our inclination and as far as our exuberance and courage will take us. The sequence leads us back to our beginnings and makes sure they're solid.

Kids

There have been two people in my classes as young as nine and a number of others between that age and eighteen. The youngest ones come with one or both parents, and their assessments of the experience range from "boring" to "I liked it" to claiming that it improved their homework and performance in sports. A family of six, all of whom were simultaneously in the class, felt their participation helped them get along better. During practice at home, the children (ages nine, ten, twelve, and fourteen) argued among themselves about the proper way and order in which to perform the movements and were forced to reach an agreement before they could proceed. Their mother discovered the sequence contributed to her calm in the midst of the inevitable chaos generated by four energetic and individualistic kids.

Dr. Lois Baron, Associate Professor of Education at Concordia University in Montreal, bought a copy of my first book, *A Potter's Notes on T'ai Chi Ch'uan,* in the fall of 1991. It's about the parallels I noticed between my practice of T'ai Chi Ch'uan and my work as a studio potter. They illuminate and reinforce each other—the ephemeral patterns of moving meditation taking concrete and practical form in clay and in the process of making a living with my art.

Based on her belief that many children today suffer from what child developmentalist David Elkind calls the "hurried child" syndrome, and moved by her own passion for and involvement with T'ai Chi Ch'uan, she designed an experiment to discover whether the practice of T'ai Chi Ch'uan could reduce anxiety and elevate self-image in grade-school students. My book motivated Lois to have the participants in the project write and draw about their experiences and responses.

Approximately fifty children were taught by a highly qualified instructor. The course included animal stances (stationary precursors of the continuously moving form), warm-up exercises, breathing procedures, a partial sequence, and some philosophical and intellectual background. The group of fifth and sixth-graders met with their "sifu" or teacher twice a week for an hour at a time over a period of twelve weeks.

At the end of the program the children filled out a questionnaire developed by Lois. The results showed that the overwhelming majority of them regarded their encounter with T'ai Chi Ch'uan as fun, easy, and—most of all—relaxing. They appreciated the slowness, softness, and "floating" quality of the movements.

I think it's surprising that kids who typically are spinning, hopping, dashing, and leaping are not only able to slow down enough to do T'ai Chi Ch'uan, but actually enjoy it and regard it as play. It is Lois' hope that T'ai Chi Ch'uan will eventually find its way into the North American school system. With the positive feedback she received from the children, we know at the very least that it can be appreciated by the young. Credit has to be given to the instructor. It's clear from what the children put on paper that he embodies the gentleness and patience a long-time practitioner acquires. "We had one of the *best* teachers (for putting up with us.)"

"When I first went," a girl writes, "I didn't like it but then it struck me. . . . I was in power. . . . When I finished T'ai Chi I felt so wonderful." This from a boy: "I like it. It's fun. I appreciate it, too. When I think of sifu our teacher I must admit I enjoy it. I enjoy it. I enjoy it some more." "My sister thought it was just stupid, but I loved it," another wrote, and went on to say, ". . . now I'm more relaxed before tests and that kind of stuff." Some of the other more interesting responses: "I never even dream of something so wonderful as T'ai Chi," "When I am nervous I use T'ai Chi," "T'ai Chi helped me to get my mind off things that I did not want to talk about," "It helps me relax for all of my sports," "It often makes me feel as if I'm flying and would never come down!"

Males

As a male in a predominantly female profession, Robin Smith experiences the tug and pull between yin and yang, feminine and masculine, every day. His work as a Family Nurse Practitioner demands he be adept at both roles as well as in the smooth transitions between them. He likes the way these contrasts are handled in the sequence—a "power movement" dissolves into a "soft movement" then emerges again into power. The more common pattern, he feels, is for assertive movements to have an abrupt and ragged finish that makes them awkward, clumsy, and unpleasant to whoever is on the receiving end. The sequence provides a different model by inextricably and gracefully linking the two opposing principles. One of the reasons Robin enjoys his work is that he likes to have physical contact with people. His healing profession gives him a "license to touch," and the sequence gives him ways to do it more sensitively.

Don Carlon finds T'ai Chi Ch'uan is a "counterpoint to the more aggressive, forceful movements inherent in the building trade." Another male who appreciates the balance offered by T'ai Chi Ch'uan is a business manager whose work requires intensity and assertiveness. Practicing the sequence helps him to be more focused and productive during working hours and affords a quiet, nurturing space after work and on the weekends.

I know some of the young boys in the class have a hard time telling their friends exactly what they're doing when they go to T'ai Chi Ch'uan class. Our culture's emphasis on machismo penetrates early to the children, and the plethora of violent movies highlighting Oriental martial arts glamorizes hand-to-hand combat. In comparison to the Bruce Lee movies, T'ai Chi Ch'uan looks like a slow and gentle dance. Parents have told me their sons emphasize to their friends that they're studying a martial art and leave the rest to their imaginations.

A friend of mine is under contract to teach movement and dance in a local elementary school. She asked me to come in to introduce T'ai Chi Ch'uan to the students. In the same conversation she mentioned that some of the boys were uncomfortable participating in something they saw as unmasculine, and that in some cases parents were reinforcing this reluctance by teasing them about the class. I realized a woman would be the wrong person to do the demonstration—I volunteered to send "a few good men" in my place. I view the teaching and learning and practicing of T'ai Chi Ch'uan as a stone added to the deficient side of the scale—an attempt to bring back into balance a culture that is dangerously lopsided. Too much yang and not enough yin.

About the Students

The people who come into my classes have an extensive range of motives. Some are just curious—they may stay for one session and move on to the next activity. Some come with a sense of urgency, looking for ways to cope with physical or psychological crises or with chronic problems. Others are looking to expand their understanding of the martial arts. And there are those who are looking for new ways to know themselves.

Probably a majority of people in the classes have backgrounds in or are currently practicing other martial arts or forms of meditation. (I get quite a few refugees from the hard martial arts who are tired of the roughness or who have sustained injuries in those practices that prohibit them from continuing.) As a group they tend to be aware of the body's basic needs when it comes to maintaining and regaining health—proper nutrition, adequate rest, exercise, and a fulfilling life. T'ai Chi Ch'uan is one part of a thoughtful lifestyle aimed at training and developing their minds and bodies.

A number of people have told me they want to meditate but have a hard time sitting still. So T'ai Chi Ch'uan, which combines movement with meditation, is their solution. One such person used weaving for years as a means of attaining an inner quiet and now also has the sequence for that purpose. T'ai Chi Ch'uan can be an excellent prelude to seated meditation—it ushers us into a state of alertness and tranquillity. (My mornings frequently start with a three-mile run followed by T'ai Chi Ch'uan and then meditation—a progression from vigorous activity to utter stillness.)

I make a point of telling people in the first class that this is not the sort of undertaking that guarantees results in three weeks—it's a long-term pursuit, ideally spanning years, decades—which brings steady and gradually accruing rewards. Still, it's not unusual for people to tell me they notice immediate benefits. For some it's a case of love at first sight—T'ai Chi Ch'uan can be a perfect fit and precisely the implement a person has been looking for. One woman writes, "I felt from the first day that I was coming home to the movements—that the 'dance' of T'ai Chi was very familiar and even comforting. . . . I practice the sequence every morning as part of my transition ritual between being asleep and awake—and the occasional days when I don't get to I feel 'off' and uncentered all day."

One of the long-term rewards for me as a practitioner and teacher is to get the sort of feedback I've recorded here. People devise delightfully inventive ways of applying the patterns and principles of T'ai Chi Ch'uan to their lives. Yet this is a very natural and probably unavoidable result of diligent practice—the sequence becomes part of them, goes where they go and does what they do.

The true value of the art is in how people weave it into their everyday activities. It makes a difference—draws us up to new levels—and generates a ripple effect through our environment. I try to impress on people that each practice is like a drop in the bucket, even on the days of less than perfect concentration. A slight change in attitude or approach brought about by practicing T'ai Chi Ch'uan day after day adds up to a significantly changed and improved life.

I have a favorite image from my interviews that places T'ai Chi Ch'uan inside a person who is inside a much larger landscape and illustrates the heightened communication and appreciation between the two. A woman told me her most memorable experience with the sequence was when she rose at sunrise while camping in the wilderness of the Trinity Alps. White granite slopes dotted with wiry manzanita surrounded her as she practiced—naked except for her hiking boots.

T'ai Chi Ch'uan in the Mountains